The Raggedy Ann and Andy

Family Album

by Susan Ann Garrison

4880 Lower Valley Rd. Atglen, PA 19310 USA

Acknowledgments

First I wish to thank Gwen Daniels, who from a great distance encouraged the completion of this book. Her photos were a needed shot in the arm, for which I am grateful.

When I wasn't really sure which end was up in terms of photography, Lori Kleuskens appeared to share her expertise. She traveled quite a distance on many occasions to take pictures and lend support.

A special thank-you goes to Janie Stock, who always has been there to lend her support. She believed in this project from the beginning.

Much love to Worth, Sue and Kim Gruelle for their continued support, concern and encouragement of this project.

Thanks go to Karen Bondi and Leslie Wesley from Applause Company for valuable information.

My greatest appreciation is extended to Gwen Daniels, Candy Brainard, Barbara and Ray Dubay, Jo Keiser, Kathy George, Helen Gibboney, Patricia Snyder, Barbara McConnell, Jane Stock, Barbara and Bob Lauver, Nancy McGlamery and Ed Pelton, and Michael Barnett for use of their photographs.

And finally, last but not least, a very special thank-you to Nancy Schiffer for her tireless creativity, energy, and expert assistance in making this book a reality.

Revised Price Guide: 1998
Copyright © 1989 by Susan Ann Garrison.
Library of Congress Catalog Number: 89-84172.

Printed in the United States of America.
ISBN: 0-7643-0468-2

Dedication

With great joy I dedicate this book to Worth Gruelle, whose talent as an illustrator and cartoonist has been a gift to all of us. Aside from illustrating six of the major Raggedy Ann books written by his father, Johnny Gruelle, he has been the overseer of all Raggedy production for the past fifty years! We are thankful to him and his wonderful family.

Preface

The main objective of this book is to familiarize the reader with the variety of commercially made Raggedy Anns and Raggedy Andys produced over the past seventy years. This is primarily a picture book of the Raggedys developed from the basic desire to share with others the love of and fascination with these dolls. All items in this book are from the collection of the author unless otherwise noted.

This book may be used as a guide to some of the dolls still available at shows and flea markets; but by no means claims to be an inclusive authority.

"What adventures you must have had, Raggedy. What joy and happiness you have brought into this world. And no matter what treatment you have received, how patient you have been! What lessons of kindness and fortitude you might teach could you talk; you with your wisdom of years. No wonder rag dolls are best beloved! You are so kindly, so patient, so lovable."

--Quote from Raggedy Ann's Stories

Contents

Introduction

Maybe there is no rational explanation for the popularity of Raggedy Ann and Andy over the last seventy years. These soft, "smiley-faced," lovable dolls have found their way into the hearts and homes of millions worldwide.

Raggedys seem to fit in just about anywhere--they're not fussy. They can sit up, lie down, lean on one arm, or roll up in a ball without the least amount of difficulty! They can fly through the air or tumble down a flight of stairs and remain unscathed. If an arm mysteriously disappears, it can be reconstructed and resown without any pain or discomfort. They just keep on smiling throughout all the turmoil of growing up.

As Marcella, the oldest of John and Myrtle Gruelle's three children, was growing up in Norwalk, Connecticut, she suffered a long and painful illness resulting from a contaminated Smallpox vaccination. She spent many hours of her short life playing with her dolls. When Marcella found an old, worn rag doll in her grandmother's attic, Gruelle, a professional illustrator and cartoonist, painted a face on it and named her by combining the titles of two poems by James Whitcomb Riley: "The Raggedy Man" and "Orphan Annie." Raggedy Ann became Marcella's constant companion. Johnny Gruelle made up stories about Raggedy Ann to tell and amuse his children. Through the stories he sought relief from the pain of his daughter's suffering by wandering into a fantasy world where dolls come to life, have real feelings, and share magical experiences. The secret was that the dolls would move about only after everyone else in the house was asleep.

When Marcella died in 1916, very little was said or done by Gruelle to deal with the loss of his only daughter. The personality of Marcella and her nursery of toys and dolls is the basic setting for many of the Gruelle books, even though, at the time they were published, the child no longer was living.

The patent date on Raggedy Ann's design is 1915 (see page 7). Clearly, Gruelle intended to protect his ownership of the Raggedy Ann idea from this time forward. Gruelle put on paper the words he had vocalized so often during Marcella's illness and made charming illustrations to accompany the stories. Beginning with *The Raggedy Ann Stories*, published in 1918, he wrote 25 books in the series and illustrated many other children's books before his untimely death on January 10, 1938, in Miami Springs, Florida.*

Marcella's Stories, published in 1929, was Johnny Gruelle's final and greatest effort to put his feelings for his daughter on paper. This book outsold all other books written for children in the 1920s.

It was Johnny Gruelle's belief that the happy smile of a Raggedy Ann could bring joy to any child's face. This magical theory has proven itself thousands--if not millions--of times since the character's conception.

*Johnny Gruelle was born on Christmas day in 1888.

Reproduction of the original patent design for Raggedy Ann.

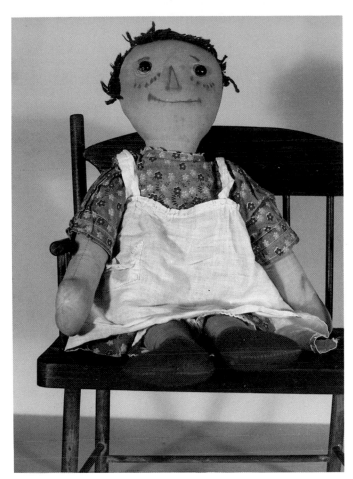

15-in (38-cm) very early Raggedy Ann. This doll is most probably one of the early "Cottage" dolls made by hand. Note the irregular eyelashes, eyebrows, and mouth. 1918-1924. Kathy George Collection.

The P. F. Volland Company, the first distributor of Johnny Gruelle's first book, *The Raggedy Ann Stories,* requested the author to make dolls of his main character to help sell the books. So the various members of Johnny's close-knit family, using as a prototype the old family doll originally made by one of the grandmothers--no one is sure who--produced a few dozen dolls. Both grandmothers, Aunt Prudence, and Uncle Justin helped Johnny, Myrtle, and sons Worth and Richard. In their home town of Norwalk, a family friend owned a shirt-making factory which was idle part of the year. Here the Gruelles used a fourth-floor space with rows of sewing machines to make the first dolls and clothing. Uncle Justin (who later illustrated *Betsy Bonnet String*) and Johnny painted most of the faces. Aunt Prudence had a rubber stamp dated 1917 which she used to identify the dolls she completed.

Johnny's five-year-old son, Worth, had the most important job of all. He would be sent to the ground floor of the factory building to a candy shop to buy candy hearts that said "I Love You" to put into each doll. When the store owner became distressed at the sight of Worth's sticky hands going through his candy hearts, Worth was given a nickel to buy a bag of hearts and do his own searching.

From late in 1918 the Gruelle family licensed the P. F. Volland Company to arrange for the manufacturing of Raggedy Ann dolls. Since that time a few carefully chosen manufacturers have been licensed to make the dolls, and one company made a version of the dolls without securing legal rights to Gruelle's design. These events are explained further in the following chapters.

The subtle variety of faces, hair styles, clothing, and proportions of the Raggedy Ann family of dolls makes great fun of comparing with another. Each company made recognizable changes--all based on Johnny Gruelle's original design--but with their own distinctive interpretations.

Another of the charming story friends to become a manufactured doll was Beloved Belindy. Later, their pal the Camel with the Wrinkled Knees, also became a doll. These latter two dolls do not appear nearly as often as Ann or Andy or in as many variations.

Over the years, thousands and perhaps millions of toys and dolls have come and gone as the fad of that moment dictated, but the dear Raggedys have held their own. Regardless of the country's economic situation or changes in attitudes and style, Raggedy Ann and Andy have maintained their instant and consistent appeal.

Raggedy's shining, smiling face has been present in some of the most unexpected places. In 1966 Ann and Andy traveled all the way to Monaco to help with the country's one-hundredth anniversary. (Princess Grace from Philadelphia had a Raggedy Andy as a child.) A year later over 250 Raggedys were present at the U.S. Pavilion at the Montreal Expo, and were honored as "the classic American folk doll."

According to a *Time* magazine article in 1969:

> Even in Vietnam, homeless and parentless children from the war...came under the spell of the doll with the universal face. The excitement caused by the arrival of gum, candy bars, and Raggedy Ann dolls to this bombed-out village "Vo Dat" is unbelievable.... The boys in the hospital here, even the teens, hug the dolls without shame. These are the same boys who are experts at carrying rifles and who are quite familiar with money-changing, black marketeering, etc.

Bob Hope took several Raggedys to the GIs overseas when he went on tour, and several old news photos show Caroline Kennedy with her Ann. Another president's daughter, Margaret Truman, insisted that her Raggedy Ann be donned in a new dress so that she would be "acceptable" to meet Washington society when her father was elected to the Senate in 1934.

While it has been our hope to show all the major variations of these dolls, we know there are others out there we have not yet met. This family is much bigger than we guessed when we started to take their pictures. We have met some in collectors' homes, at toy and doll shows, and sometimes when we're thinking about something else altogether! When the readers meet a member of Raggedy Ann's family not included in this book, we hope they will send the author a picture in care of the publisher for the next Family Album. We want everyone to be a part of the fun.

P. F. Volland Company 1920-1934

The P. F. Volland Company was the original publisher and distributor of Johnny Gruelle's children's books. After *Raggedy Ann Stories* was published in 1917, the question arose, "Where's the doll?" To answer the question, members of the Gruelle family banded together and made about three dozen dolls (see page 7). Then a request came from Marshall Fields Department Store in Chicago to use the dolls to promote book sales.

During this time the Gruelle family licensed the P. F. Volland Company to arrange larger-scale manufacturing of Raggedy Ann dolls. Two years later, after the Raggedy Andy book was published, Volland also arranged for the Andy dolls to be made.

The earliest manufactured Raggedys distributed by Volland were 15 inches (38 cm) to 16 inches (41 cm) tall and had brown or auburn hair that usually was sparse or did not cover the back of the head. The feet turned outward. Very early Andy had slightly longer legs to accommodate the pants. Hands often were oversized and some had very large thumbs. Ann's peasant dress, in subtle colors, had a small ruffle at the neck. Pantaloons and a pinafore completed her outfit.

Early Raggedy Ann has a copyright date of September 7, 1915, found printed on the torso. As illustrated on the original copyrighted pattern of 1915, Ann was supposed to have a very thin nose, a puffy skirt, and a hat. It is obvious that these dolls are not the ones produced by P. F. Volland Company, but no evidence could be found to validate the change in design.

16-in (41-cm) Raggedy Ann, P.F. Volland Co. Shoe button eyes, painted nose and mouth, brown yarn hair, replaced dress. Patent date: September 7, 1915. 1920-1934. Gwen Daniels Collection.

Collection of the author.

16-in (41-cm) Raggedy Ann, P.F. Volland Co. Thicker eyebrows and lovely dress fabric. Candy Brainard Collection.

Unlike Andy's present-day outfit, the earlier ones had a separate shirt and pants. Buttons are found in the back as well as the front (at the waist). The pieces often were stitched together, which may have been an aid in saving the original clothes. Many of the earlier faces with shoe button eyes have faded, but there still are several good examples in various collections. P. F. Volland Company went out of business in 1934, and ceased manufacturing the dolls at that time.

Exposition Toy and Doll Company then continued the Raggedy production, but production lasted less than a year because of the strong competition from Mollye Goldman.

15-in (38-cm) Raggedy Andy, P.F. Volland Co., late 1920s. Note large thumbs. Barbara and Roy Dubay Collection.

Close-up of the Volland Andy. Replaced hat. Barbara and Roy Dubay Collection.

Below is a group portrait of Volland dolls from the Candy Brainard Collection. There are several variations in eyelashes, noses, and mouths.

15-in (38-cm) Raggedy Ann by P.F. Volland Co. Shoe button eyes, painted nose and mouth, brown yarn hair. Hat is missing. 1920s. Gwen Daniels Collection.

Gwen Daniels Collection. Here we have a comparison study of a few Volland Raggedy Andys. There are variations in eyebrows, noses, mouths, hand size, and leg stripes. All three outfits are slightly different. The mouth above, with the larger red area in the center, was a favorite of Johnny Gruelle. 1920-1934.

This Andy is riding an early Fisher Price horse. Note that he has no lower lashes. Patricia Snyder Collection.

16-in (41-cm) Raggedy Ann, P.F. Volland Co. Replaced apron and pantaloons, brown feet. September 7, 1915 stamped on back torso. Barbara and Roy Dubay Collection.

Close-up of the Volland Ann. Sweet, knowing face. These small facial tears are very common with dolls of this age. Barbara and Roy Dubay Collection.

15-in (38-cm) Andy by P.F. Volland Company. Mint condition. Wider leg stripes. Notice the closeness of the lower lashes. 1920-1938.

15-in (38-cm) Beloved Belindy by P.F. Volland Co. Original. Missing collar, scarf, apron, and pantaloons. 1920s. Jo Keiser Collection.

15-in (38-cm) Beloved Belindy by P.F. Volland Co. All original. Candy Brainard Collection.

15-in (38-cm) Beloved Belindy by P.F. Volland Co. Unmarked. Legs replaced, very faint lines for teeth on the mouth. Top and bottom of the dress are sewn together. Organdy apron, original outfit, black cloth body. 1920s. Gwen Daniels Collection.

16-in (41-cm) Raggedy Ann and Andy by P.F. Volland Co. Heads have been reworked with other fabric, embroidery, hair, and eyes. Bodies and all clothes but the pinafore seem original, so probably this repair was done many years ago. 1920s. Gwen Daniels Collection.

Raggedy Ann by Exposition Doll and Toy Co. When Volland went out of business, this company was given the legal right and patent to continue with the Raggedy production. They were in business less than a year, from late 1934 to the middle of 1935, because the competition from Mollye Goldman was too strong. I am very grateful to Patricia Snyder for sharing this photo with us. It was the "missing link" I thought never would be found!

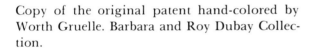

Copy of the original patent hand-colored by Worth Gruelle. Barbara and Roy Dubay Collection.

14 1/2-in (37-cm) Andy. Unmarked, mint condition, painted features on oil cloth, red checkered shirt, blue pants and hat, yellow stick-on buttons at waist. No date. Gwen Daniels Collection.

15-in (38-cm) "Buddy" by American Toy and Novelty Mfg. Co. Inc. Oil cloth face, auburn hair, removable pants and hat. Unmarked. Date unknown.

14 1/2-in (37-cm) Andy. Oil cloth, red and white checkered legs. A well-loved example of the doll pictured above. Company unknown; unmarked. Note resemblance to the face on the original patent! Gwen Daniels Collection.

15-in (38-cm) Raggedy copies. Andy is tagged: "I'm Buddy/Huggable Nursery Pet, American Toy and Novelty Mfg. Co. Inc." Oil cloth faces and rough cotton bodies. Ann has removable skirt and pantaloons. Andy has removable pants and hat. Each doll is made from seven different fabrics. No date. Little Brother by Effanbee Co., original 1940s.

16-in (41-cm) Andy-type boy by American Toy and Novelty Mfg. Co. Inc. Oil cloth face, yarn hair partially covering the back of the head. Hat and shirt are replacements; original outfit is underneath. Unmarked. 1940s. Barbara and Roy Dubay Collection.

15-in (38-cm) pair of oil-cloth-faced dolls by American Toy and Novelty Co. Wild outfits! Date unknown. Collection of Bob and Barbara Lauver.

15-in (38-cm) Raggedy Ann and Andy, American Toy and Novelty Mfg. Co. Inc. Oil cloth faces, rough cotton body, torso and blouse caps are attached, missing skirt. Andy's pants and hat are removable. Unmarked. Date unknown. Gwen Daniels Collection.

Hearts

A woman in Connecticut remembers going to sleep as a child with her original pair of Raggedy dolls. She recalls sucking on the chests of both dolls to taste the candy hearts inside, and years later seeing the stains still there was a reminder of that contented period of childhood.

From the information collected so far, it is believed that the P. F. Volland Company dolls originally had candy hearts placed inside their chests. When parents complained that the dolls would get sticky, the hearts were removed. Then there were complaints that Ann had no heart. The answer is believed to have been the use of cardboard hearts as substitutes.

In 1935 Mollye Goldman was the first manufacturer to imprint a heart on Ann's chest--a solid red one. By this date, Andy had a heart, too. (It is believed that candy hearts were stuck to the outside of the chests of early dolls avoid the stain problem, but this information has not been verified.) Since then Ann and Andy have had printed hearts that say "I Love You."

14-in (36-cm) Mollye Baby by Mollye Goldman. Reddish orange hair, painted face, blue flowered arms and torso fabric. Green print dress, multicolored legs, blue feet. Mint. Unmarked, 1935-1938. 18-in (46-cm) Mollye pair. Written on chest: "Raggedy Ann and Andy Dolls Manufactured by Mollye's Doll Outfitters." Andy has painted face, blue print shirt, blue pants, shoes, hat. Ann has blue flowered dress, white organdy apron, blue shoes, white pantaloons. Mint, 1935-1938. Gwen Daniels Collection.

Raggedy Andy by Mollye. Tagged on chest as above. Multicolored legs; blue shirt, pants, and feet. Nose outlined in black. Original. 1935-1938. Gwen Daniels Collection.

Close-up of Mollye Baby.

Mollye Goldman 1935-1938

Contrary to information previously in print, the connection between Mollye Goldman, the Gruelle family, and the world of Raggedys was less than positive. Within a year after the Volland Company ceased production of the dolls in 1934, Mollye Goldman began making her version of Raggedy Ann and Andy under the name of Mollye's Doll Outfitters. The February 1936 *Playthings* showed an illustration of Mollye's dolls with the following information: "May 7, 1935 design patent was filed for Andy No. 96,382. Other patents were 363,226 and 56,711 for Andy, and 363,008 for Ann." These were made without the permission of the Gruelle family, who always has held the rights to the dolls regardless of the company involved. A year before, in the May issue of *Playthings*, the Johnny Gruelle Co. defended their patent as being the only legitimate one, indicating that both dolls were registered with the U.S. Patent Office with number 107,328, dated November 23, 1915.

Even though she was confronted with the illegality of her action, she refused to stop making the dolls. An immediate lawsuit ensued to stop her production. For three years the Gruelle family, headed by Johnny's wife, Myrtle, used legal assistance--including lawyers representing Georgene Novelties Co. Inc. in New York--to stop Mollye Goldman.

It is reported that she made over a million dollars on the Raggedys alone before the Supreme Court ruled in favor of Myrtle Gruelle in 1938. That is why the Mollye's Doll Outfitters' Raggedy Ann and Raggedy Andy were only in production from 1935 to 1938.

One might assume that since the Mollye Raggedys were such a radical change from the Volland Dolls, it should be all right to make them. However, two things are wrong here: (1) using the names "Raggedy Ann" and "Raggedy Andy," and (2) failing to obtain permission. If Mollye had decided on any other name but "Raggedy," this court case never would have taken place.

14-in (36-cm) Baby Ann by Mollye Goldman. Flat oil cloth face, black outlined nose, auburn hair. Back of head is round and the same fabric as the torso. Sleeve caps and removable skirt, organdy apron and pantaloons.
14-in (36-cm) Baby Andy by Mollye Goldman. Face, head, and feet the same as Ann. Different stripes on legs. Both unmarked, 1935-1938. Author's Collection.

21-in (53-cm) Raggedy Ann by Mollye Goldman. Apron added. This doll still has her original box. Body like Andy on the previous page. 1935-1938. Kathy George Collection.

Close-up of the Mollye pair. 1935-1938. Gwen Daniels Collection.

22-in (55-cm) Raggedy Ann by Mollye. Missing apron and pantaloons. Kathy George Collection.

21-in(53-cm) Ann by Mollye. Replaced outfit. Gwen Daniels Collection.

Group portrait of Mollye's Raggedys from the Candy Brainard Collection.

Georgene Novelties Company, Inc. 1938-1962

In 1938 the Gruelle family entered an agreement with the Georgene Novelties Co., Inc. in New York for the manufacture of Raggedy dolls for the next 25 years. Both Ann and Andy dolls now had a thick head of hair, and Ann had a distinguished top knot that helped to differentiate her from Andy. The yarn ranged in color from a deep, pinkish-red auburn in the beginning to all shades of orange and even dirty blonde.

The Georgene Company's mouths were more defined, with a definite red center, and exhibited six different expressions, depending on the size of the doll and when it was produced.

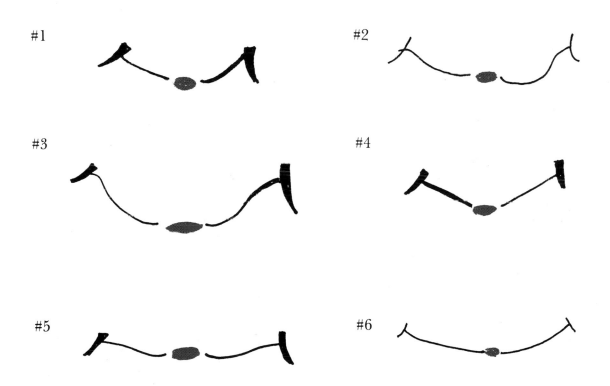

Early on, Georgene tin eyes were attached by thread sewn through to the back of the head. Later eyes are plastic and protrude slightly from the face.

Noses were originally long, as on the Volland-made dolls. However, they were large, more defined, deeper red, and outlined in black. They evolved into a triangular shape with no black outline and usually were orange.

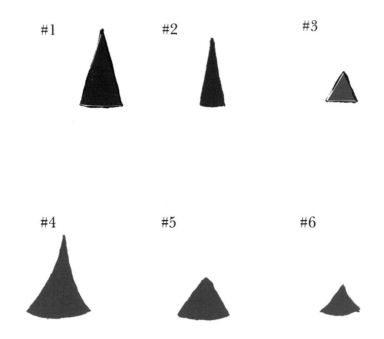

All Georgenes have seams in the middle of the legs and arms to represent knees and elbows. Feet face forward, except for the Awake-Asleep dolls where the toes turn outward. Legs are mainly red-and-white striped, but variations have been found, such as blue-and-white checked, blue-and-white striped, red-and-white dots, and stripes going the "wrong way."

The hearts on the left side of the front torso vary from a very crude, almost handpainted look to a large, well-defined shape. All of these dolls have hearts.

Georgene Novelties Co. Inc. Tags and Labels

These tags are found sewn into the left side seam.

A

> JOHNNY GRUELLE'S OWN
> RAGGEDY ANN AND ANDY DOLLS
> Trademark Reg. U.S. Patent Off.
> Copyright 1918-1920 by John B. Gruelle
> ———————————
> GEORGENE NOVELTIES, INC.
> NEW YORK CITY
> EXCLUSIVE LICENSED MANUFACTURERS
> MADE IN U.S.A.

B

> JOHNNY GRUELLE'S OWN
> RAGGEDY ANN AND ANDY DOLLS
> Copyright, P.F. Volland Co. 1918, 1920
> Copyright Renewed, Myrtle T. Gruelle 1945,
> 1947 ———————————
> GEORGENE NOVELTIES, INC.
> NEW YORK CITY
> EXCLUSIVE LICENSED MANUFACTURERS
> MADE IN U.S.A.

C

> JOHNNY GRUELLE'S OWN
> RAGGEDY ANN AND ANDY DOLLS
> Copyright P. F. Volland Co. 1918, 1920,
> 1925, 1926: John B. Gruelle 1924, 1928,
> 1930, 1931, 1932, 1935, 1937; Copyright
> renewed Myrtle Gruelle 1945, 1947
> ———————————
> GEORGENE NOVELTIES, INC.
> NEW YORK CITY
> Exclusive Licensed Manufacturers
> MADE IN U.S.A.

D

> JOHNNY GRUELLE'S OWN
> RAGGEDY ANN AND ANDY DOLLS
> CHARACTER CREATED and Copr.
> By John B. Gruelle 1918-1937
> Copyright 1946 By Myrtle Gruelle Silsby
> ———————————
> GEORGENE NOVELTIES, INC.
> NEW YORK CITY
> Exclusive Licensed Manufacturers
> MADE IN U.S.A.

Betty McConnell Collection.

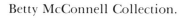

Author's Collection.

19-in (48-cm). Here are three of the earliest Georgene Raggedys in their original outfits. All have long noses outlined in black. Andy on the left has tin buttons on the front of his shirt and at the waist. TAG A.

Close-up of the early Georgene pair. 1938-1945.

Kathy George Collection.

This is an ad found in a 1941 Saturday Evening Post. These are examples of dolls which were given free for a subscription to the magazine!

19-in (48-cm) early Georgene Raggedy Andy. This little guy has on the same outfit as the Saturday Evening Post advertisement. His yarn hair is slightly darker than many of the dolls from this era. 1940-1945. Barbara and Roy Dubay Collection.

19-in (48-cm) early pair by Georgene Novelties Co., Inc. Ann's outfit has been attractively replaced in the style of the period. Andy is original, missing his hat. They are sitting on an early Schoenhut piano. Barbara and Roy Dubay Collection.

Close-up of Georgene Raggedy Ann. TAG A. 19-in

19" (48-cm) early pair by Georgene Novelties Co. all original. This pair by Georgene is enjoying their afternoon in the sun.

19" (48-cm) early pair by Georgene, all original. Notice the spacing of the leg stripes on these and Ann's dress is an almost identical match to those on the Mallyes—see page 24. Barbara and Bob Lauver Collection.

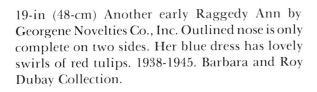
(48-cm) pair by Georgene Novelties Co., Inc. Barbara and Roy Dubay Collection.

Full view of the doll. TAG A.

19-in (48-cm) Another early Raggedy Ann by Georgene Novelties Co., Inc. Outlined nose is only complete on two sides. Her blue dress has lovely swirls of red tulips. 1938-1945. Barbara and Roy Dubay Collection.

This perky pair of original Raggedys also are Georgenes of the same period.
19-in (48-cm) all original Andy has been loved so much they kissed his lips right off! His outfit is similar to that of the Andy on the pony, but his hair is auburn. 1938-1945. Kathy George Collection.

50-in (127-cm) Raggedy Andy by Georgene Novelties Co., Inc. This wonderfully large doll probably was made specially for a large department store display. He would be used for a centerpiece and the smaller dolls would be clustered around him. He has no heart, while the smaller outline noses all seem to have hearts, except for the Awake-Asleep dolls. His outfit is original and includes painted white metal buttons down the paneled shirt and on the pant legs as well. He is missing his hat. 1938-1945.

Awake Asleep

12-in (31-cm) Awake-Asleep pair of Raggedys by Georgene Novelties Co., Inc. Smaller version of the usually 15-in (38-cm) size. All original. Neither has a heart. Ann's red and white legs continue to form the lower portion of the torso. Ann has a red tag; Andy has a blue one. Hair is found only at the head side seam. TAG A. Barbara and Roy Dubay Collection.

15-in (38-cm) Awake-Asleep Raggedy Ann and Andy by Georgene Novelties Co., Inc. Black outlined noses. (Not all of these dolls had the black outline.) Original outfits. Cutie pies! TAG A, 1938-1950. Gwen Daniels Collection.

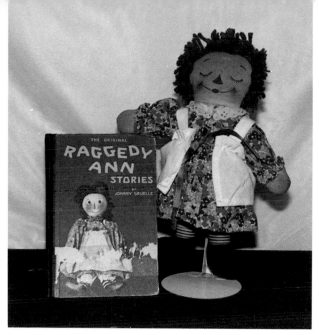

15-in (38-cm) Awake-Asleep Raggedy Ann by Georgene Novelties Co., Inc. Although she has the same dress as the previous Ann, her face has the feel of oil cloth and legs are blue instead of red.

The yarn hair also is different. Replaced pinafore. TAG A, 1938-1945. Raggedy Ann Stories by Johnny Gruelle, M.A. Donohue, 1918.

12-in (31-cm) Raggedy Andy by Georgene Novelties Co., Inc. His heart tag is on his "Awake" side, but he preferred to close his eyes in the bright light! TAG A, 1938-1950. Collection of Bob and Barbara Lauver.

15-in (38-cm) Awake-Asleep Raggedy Andy, Georgene Novelties Co., Inc. This doll was loved so much his face is almost gone and he has a toupee to cover his bald head! For some reason, these often are found in a worn condition. 1938-1945. Private Collection.

20-in (51-cm) early Georgene Ann in a lovely pink outfit. Barbara and Roy Dubay Collection.

23-in (59-cm) early Raggedy Ann from Georgene Novelties Co., Inc. Flowered feet to match dress. Thin-striped legs. Beautiful hair. TAG A, 1938-1945. Compare to handmade Ann. Creator must have done his or her best to duplicate the commercially made doll. All original. Probably late 1930s.

19-in (48-cm) early Raggedy Andy from Georgene Novelties Co., Inc. Very attractive suit with a plaid top, painted metal buttons, thin-striped legs, brown hair. He insisted upon wearing his bunny slippers for this portrait! TAG A, 1938-1950.

19-in (48-cm) Raggedy Andy by Georgene Novelties Co., Inc. Thick orange hair, early paneled shirt, and his "wrong way" leg stripes are of a much thicker textured fabric than normal. TAG A, 1938-1950.

20-in (51-cm) Raggedy Andy from Georgene Novelties Co., Inc. This fellow is an earlier doll, evident by the hair, paneled shirt, and tin buttons. Blue-checked legs and a solid blue hat of the same material as the pants. Missing tag, 1938-1950.

23-in (58-cm) Raggedy Ann by Georgene Novelties Co., Inc. Same as Andy doll, except for blue and white legs. Our little musician! TAG A, 1938-1945. Gwen Daniels Collection.

22-in (56-cm) Raggedy Andy by Georgene Novelties Co., Inc. TAG D. What a personality! Obviously mate to Ann, but legs are different color. 1938-1945. Gwen Daniels Collection.

19-in (48-cm) mint pair of Georgene Raggedys from the early 1940s. These beautiful dolls have lovely burnt orange hair and noses usually found on larger dolls of this period. Their heart paper tags are unusual because the only dates printed are 1918 on Ann and 1922 on Andy. Also, the tin buttons on Andy's shirt and the back of Ann's skirt are painted bright red instead of the usual white. TAG A, 1940-1945. Collection of Nancy McGlamery and Ed Pelton.

19-in (48-cm) unusual pair by Georgene Novelties Co., Inc. Ann has thin-blue-striped legs that match his shirt. Their friend is a little "Bossy Bull" toy by Fisher Price. 1938-1950. Barbara and Roy Dubay Collection.

23-in (58-cm) Raggedy Anns by Georgene Novelties Co., Inc. Button eyes tied through the head, thin-striped legs, flowered feet that match the dress. Believed to be the first 23-inch size by this company. TAG A. Beautiful workmanship. 1938-1950.

18-in (46-cm) Andy by Georgene. Red-dotted legs, painted tin buttons on pants. Original. TAG A, 1938-1945. Gwen Daniels Collection.

When these Raggedys were told to line up to get their pictures taken, they decided this arrangement was a lot more interesting!

Opposite page:
15-in (38-cm) Raggedy Andy by Georgene Novelties Co., Inc. Every now and then we come across a Knickerbocker or Georgene doll that is made from two front torso pieces. After noticing the heart on this doll's back, it took a while to realize that not only was the heart there, but an entire face was underneath the hair. This little Andy is one of these special dolls, but I didn't want to remove the hair. TAG C, 1938-1962.

24-in (61-cm) pair by Georgene Novelties Co., Inc. that has undergone some repair. Andy has a replaced left arm, and Ann's ordeal is described at the beginning of the book (page ..). She is holding a little 6-inch pair of Knickerbockers. TAG B for Andy, no tag for Ann. 1938-1962.

19-in (48-cm) My only example of this early Georgene with an unusual nose. Replaced right eye. He looks like a boy, but that's only a guess. No tag. 1938-1950.

15-in (38-cm) Raggedy Anns and Andys by Georgene Novelties Co., Inc. All original outfits. Ann has a prominent top knot. This small size often has a long, flat mouth instead of the characteristic smile. The boys enjoy their English handmade wool bear companion, while the girls below play with an Applause "stuffy." All TAG B except Andy in blue has a flesh-colored tag that reads "KIRGET." 1938-1962.

A lovely display of Georgene Raggedys from the Barbara and Roy Dubay Collection.

15-in (38-cm) Raggedy Anns from Georgene Novelties Co., Inc. This pair really shows how sweet some of the smaller dolls can be. Ann on the left has TAG C, which indicates a copyright renewal by Myrtle Gruelle in 1945 and 1947. Ann on right has TAG D, which states the copyright held by Myrtle Gruelle Silsby in 1946. (Maybe their tags are different because their mouths are different?) 1946-1963.

15-in (38-cm) Raggedy Ann by Georgene Novelties Co., Inc. Pink flowered dress. TAG B, 1938-1962. Private collection.

15-in (38-cm) Raggedy Anns by Georgene Novelties Co., Inc. Fabric pattern of the dress on the right really is quite unusual. TAG C. Barbara and Roy Dubay Collection.

19-in (48-cm) "Suzy Ann." She is the fattest Georgene Raggedy I've ever seen! TAG C, 1938-1952.

16-in (41-cm) Raggedy Andy by Georgene Novelties Co., Inc. All original. Note the placement of the center of the mouths on each of these. TAG C, 1938-1962.

Our little tree climber on the left and the Andy with the two hearts on the right.

15-in (38-cm) Raggedy Andy by Georgene Novelties Co., Inc. When this little guy saw the camera, he headed for the nearest tree because he has flowers on his shirt instead of the usual checks! No tag, 1938-1962.

15-in (38-cm) Raggedy Ann by Georgene Novelties Co., Inc. Ann has had a tear in her forehead repaired from the inside of the head with an iron-on patch. The cotton stuffing still had the seeds in it! Original outfit. Hair replaced. TAG B, 1938-1962.

19-in (48-cm) pair by Georgene. Ann's dress has yellow and orange flowers. Replaced pinafore. TAG C, Andy has TAG B. 1938-1962.

15-in (38-cm) pair from Georgene Novelties Co., Inc. Right lines of the mouth are straight and run into the red center section. Dotted shirt on Andy; flowered dress on Ann. TAG B, 1938-1962.

19-in (48-cm) pair of orange-haired Raggedys by Georgene. Ann has a blue flowered dress and Andy's shirt is an interesting purple, green, and white print. TAG C, 1938-1962. Barbara and Roy Dubay Collection.

While their sisters and brothers were being photographed, these two Georgene Annies insisted upon playing Hide-and-Seek!

15-in (38-cm) Raggedy Ann by Georgene Novelties Co., Inc. Another dress print. All original. TAG C, 1938-1962. Barbara and Roy Dubay Collection.

15-in (38-cm) Raggedy Andy by Georgene Novelties Co., Inc. with an interesting shirt. TAG C. Barbara and Roy Dubay Collection.

Johnny Gruelle felt that if he could share the happy smile of a Raggedy with any child, it would bring joy. How often over the years has a crying child broken into a smile when shown the face of a Raggedy. These is something magical and peaceful about these dolls. We can share our deepest thoughts, have a shoulder to cry on, and a constant companion, all wrapped up in one! Magic-- that's the word. How else can we explain the universal appeal?

15-in (38-cm) Raggedy Ann by Georgene Novelties Co., Inc. Yellow and blue flowers match the mushrooms. Original owner has embroidered 'Little Laura' on the hem of the dress. TAG B, 1938-1962. Private Collection.

19-in (48-cm) Raggedy Andy by Georgene Novelties Co., Inc. His face is slightly soiled, but he has a handsome shirt. His friend is a nice, jointed American bear with a soft tummy. TAG C, 1938-1962.

Here are several more Raggedys by Georgene Novelties Co., Inc. All are 19-in (48-cm) except the Andy to the far right. He is 15-in (38-cm) tall and has TAG B. The others have TAG C. 1938-1962. Barbara and Roy Dubay Collection.

19-in (48-cm) Raggedy Ann and Andy by Georgene Novelties Co., Inc. This mint pair still smells of cedar from being carefully stored in a trunk. They were gifts for twins but, obviously, they never touched or played with them. Andy is a fine version of the "No Hope Doll" found on page 137. TAG B. Paper heart tags read: "Johnny Gruelle's Own Raggedy Ann (Andy) Doll/Character created by Johnny Gruelle/Georgene Novelties Co., Inc., New York CityExclusive Licensed Manufacturers/Copyright 1951 by Myrtle Gruelle/Made in the U.S.A. 1951."

15-in (38-cm) pair with original tags and a 19-in (48-cm) Raggedy Ann with her original box. All are made by Georgene Novelties Co., Inc. TAG C, 1938-1962. Candy Brainard Collection.

19-in (48-cm) pair by Georgene Novelties Co., Inc. Dress has purple and blue flowers, missing pinafore. They make a sweet couple even though Annie has a dirty face. TAG B, 1938-1962.

19-in (48-cm) Georgene pair. Still another outfit in Andy. TAG B, 1938-1962.

19-in (48-cm) pair by Georgene Novelties Co., Inc. They are original, but took five years to find each other. Ann's blue flowered dress just matches Andy's blue checks. TAG B, 1938-1962.

19-in (48-cm) Three more Georgenes from the Barbara and Roy Dubay Collection.

19-in (48-cm) pair with the same facial expression, but different hair styles. Barbara and Roy Dubay Collection.

19-in (48-cm) Raggedy Ann and Andy from Georgene Novelties Co., Inc. Replaced suit and pantaloons. Ann loves her knitted sandals. Many times pairs were found with different hair color. Andy often was referred to as the "little red-headed brother." TAG B, 1938-1962.

19-in (48-cm) Raggedy Ann from Georgene Novelties Co., Inc. This sweet little girl in an uncommon pink dress truly is beautiful. One can imagine her as a great listener and companion. TAG B, 1938-1962.

19-in (48-cm) Raggedy Anns. MIDDLE: 15-in (38-cm) Ann. All by Georgene. They just couldn't resist an afternoon tea party. TAG C, 1938-1962.

19-in (48-cm) Raggedy Ann from Georgene Novelties Co., Inc. Dress of green, blue, yellow, and orange flowers on white. All original. TAG B, 1938-1962.

15-in (38-cm) Raggedy Andy by Georgene Novelties Co., Inc. Original. TAG C. 19-in (48-cm) Raggedy Ann with replaced pinafore. TAG D, 1938-1962.

18 1/2-in (47-cm) Raggedy Ann and Andy by Georgene Novelties Co., Inc. They've always been together, even though the hair color is different. TAG D, 1938-1962. Gwen Daniels Collection.

15-in (38-cm) pair by Georgene Novelties Co., Inc. These, as with all dolls on this page, have the leg stripes going the "wrong way." Assuming this happens accidentally, there still are several around. TAG D, 1938-1962.

24-in (61-cm) Raggedy Ann and Andy by Georgene Novelties Co., Inc. Ann has a red and blue flowered dress. Mint condition. TAG B, 1938-1962.

23-in (59-cm) Andy by Georgene. Tin buttons, nice two-toned suit. Note rounded collar. Same as other boy, but his expression is still different. TAG C, 1938-1962. Gwen Daniels Collection.

24-in (61-cm) Georgene Andy. Replaced arm. TAG B, 1938-1962.

23'' (59-cm) Ann by Georgene. All original TAG C.

23-in (58-cm) pair by Georgene Novelties Co., Inc. Ann is totally original and has a beautiful head of hair! Andy's outfit was replaced. Eyes are different, same mouth. TAG B, 1938-1955.

19-in (48-cm) with another beautiful shirt for Andy. Ann's hair is lovely. No tags, 1938-1962. 24-in (61-cm) Raggedy Ann by Georgene.

24-in (61-cm) Raggedy Andy by Georgene Novelties Co., Inc. Replaced outfit. TAG B, 1938-1955.

36-in (91-cm) Raggedy Ann by Georgene Novel-ties Co., Inc. Dress has vertical and horizontal stripes that form squares, then flowers are pat-terned over the squares. She loved sitting in her cart at a regional doll show. TAG C, 1938-1962. Private Collection.

32-in (81-cm) pair by Georgene. Orange hair, original. TAG B, 1938-1962. Gwen Daniels Col-lection.

36-in (91-cm) Raggedy Ann by Georgene Novel-ties Co., Inc. TAG C, 1938-1962.

32-in (81-cm) pair by Georgene Novelties Co., Inc. All original. Multicolored flowered dress. Wonderful plaid shirt. TAG C. This is the pair on the title page. 1938-1962. Lamb tagged "Eden Toy Inc., N.Y. Made in Columbia."

Every mother knows the sparkling goodness of Canada Dry Ginger Ale—now surprise the family with a variety of Canada Dry's 10 tasty flavors.

Sweet Canada Dry advertisement from a 1954 Ladies Home Journal. Ann looks very much like the doll pictured above.

18-in (46-cm) Beloved Belindy by Georgene Novelties Co., Inc. Here we see two unusual additions: plastic hoop earrings and mohair around the head seam. This outfit is out of character for the Belindy we know--maybe she was on vacation! "Johnny Gruelle's Own Beloved Belindy" is imprinted faintly on the back of the head. 1938-1945. Private Collection.

Beloved Belindy

Belindy didn't mind sunbathing so that we could study her "unusual" body shape. Note tummy and hips. Great design for a cloth body.

40-in (102-cm) Belindy handmade by the author. The urge to see a huge Belindy was overwhelming, and here is the result. Her outfit is not finished, but you get the idea. She's holding a 15-in (38-cm) Georgene Ann. TAG D, 1938-1962.

Close-up of Belindy's face. Note the black mohair! I'm sure this is original.

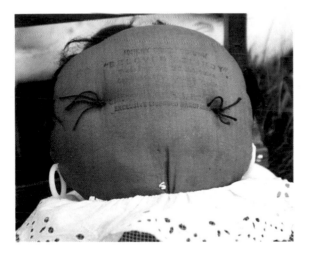

Back of Belindy's head. Many are found with no mark at all. I've read that they also stamped torsos but have not as yet seen one.

18-in (46-cm) Beloved Belindy by Georgene Novelties Co., Inc. The polka-dotted feet may be the result of fabric shortages during WW II. The bandanna may be dotted also, to match the feet. 1938-1950.

18-in (46-cm) three Beloved Belindys by Georgene Novelties Co., Inc. 1938-1950.
Pair from Candy Brainard Collection.

Yellow-gold buttons on the blouse. Kathy George Collection.

For comparison, a Knickerbocker Toy Co. Belindy on the left and a Georgene Belindy on the right. The Georgene doll is similar to the doll at the far left, but her nose isn't outlined in black, there is only one column of buttons on the blouse, and her brown color is a different shade. All original. 1938-1962.

18-in (46-cm) Beloved Belindy by Georgene. Redressed. Her legs probably have been replaced because they're solid brown and of a different shade than the rest of the body. 1938-1962. Gwen Daniels Collection.

Beloved Belindy is having a conversation with Henny Penny, the little red hen from the book *Beloved Belindy*. Author's Collection.

14 1/2-in (37-cm) Beloved Belindy by Georgene. Missing skirt, outlined nose. Printed on head: "Johnny Gruelle's Own Beloved Belindy/ Georgene Novelties Co., Inc./Exclusive Manufacturers."

Close-up of the doll.

18-in (46-cm) Beloved Belindy. What a wonderful surprise to see a doll with such beautiful eyes! The whole expression is different. She must be later, as her eyes resemble the upcoming Knickerbocker Belindy.

15-in (38-cm) Beloved Belindy by Georgene. Unmarked. Here still another face. The lack of white around the button eyes results in a strange, almost eerie look. Her sewing machine is marked "CASIGE, MADE IN GERMANY/British Zone." Barbara and Roy Dubay Collection.

McCall's printed pattern for 19-in (48-cm) dolls. Kathy George Collection.

19-in (48-cm) pair of handmades, very similar to the early Georgenes, especially the nose, eyes, and hair. Multicolored legs are reminiscent of the Mollyes that directly preceded them. Kathy George Collection.

20-in (51-cm) handmade pair. These dolls were blackened with soot and found hanging by their necks to a tree--but they had all of their clothes. They've been soaked, restuffed, and eyes were replaced. 1950s.

23-in (58-cm) handmade Awake-Asleep pair. Ann has a solid heart on her chest that says "I Luv You" in white letters. Painted faces. 1950s.

20-in (51-cm) Raggedy Ann handmade by Jonathan Greene. Cotton stuffed, brown hair, embroidered face, felt nose, feet turned outward. 1988.

22-in (56-cm) coy, mischievous-looking, handmade Raggedy has a felt nose and white felt behind the dangling button eyes. The rest of the face is embroidered. Large top knot, thumbs on the hands, and multistriped legs which have been repaired. 1930s. Gwen Daniels Collection.

30-in (76-cm) Raggedy Ann. My childhood doll made by my mother, Mary Garrison, in 1947. Her hair was quite long, but I kept trimming her braids. She has water marks on her face from all the "bottles" I gave her. Arms, legs, and torso all are connected by a single, thick-knotted string. Embroidered face.

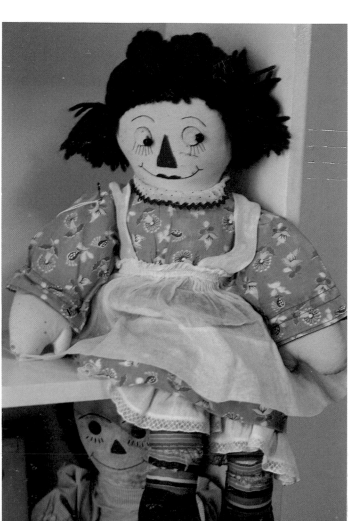

Handmade brown felt Raggedy. Beautifully embroidered face with great attention to detail. Red and white cotton legs and red felt feet. Knickerbocker outfit. Late 1960s.

20-in (51-cm) handmade Andy. When we brought him home from Massachusetts, we found a nightie under his outer clothing. It was as though he had popped out of one of the stories about Marcella dressing her dolls for bed! Bright orange hair, embroidered face, corduroy feet. 1930s. Ann, described earlier (page ..), has button eyes, auburn hair, lightly painted face, and Volland-type legs. Outfit typical of the early Georgene 24-inch dolls. 1930s.

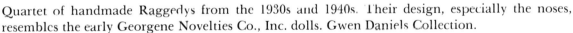

Quartet of handmade Raggedys from the 1930s and 1940s. Their design, especially the noses, resembles the early Georgene Novelties Co., Inc. dolls. Gwen Daniels Collection.

Handmade pair. Andy has black corduroy pants and feet, pink and white shirt--same as Ann's dress. Pillow ticking legs. This pair has been washed and restuffed. Eyes were replaced, embroidery resewn. Yarn was added where missing. 1930-1940s.

14 1/2-in (37-cm) Raggedy Andy. Yellow yarn hair only in the front of the head, stamped features, blue and white torso and legs. Back of head is solid red. Dressed in navy shorts and blue and white checked shirt. Maker unknown. May be unauthorized. Gwen Daniels Collection.

13-in (33-cm) handmade Andy. Nylon stocking stuffing, stenciled features. Gwen Daniels Collection.

A refinished cupboard, minus the doors, serves as a display area for some of the Knickerbocker Raggedys owned by Barbara and Roy Dubay.

I tried this. The cat had a ball, and everyone was covered with hair! Nice idea for those with a spare bedroom. Candy Brainard Collection.

Storing and displaying Raggedys can be done easily as long as the sun is taken into consideration. Cigarette smoke also will be absorbed into and eventually rot the fabric. This is a section of one room where the walls were lined to the ceiling with shelves. Author's Collection.

16-in (41-cm) Raggedy Ann. This doll has snaps around the head seam to attach her hair. There are no button eyes, but the dress is typical. It is possible that she is an unauthorized kit imported illegally into the U.S. Knickerbocker had nothing to do with the manufacturing of this doll. 1960s or 1970s.

Knickerbocker Toy Company 1962-1982

Late in 1962, Knickerbocker Toy Co. of New York City approached the Gruelle family, headed by Myrtle Gruelle, and made an offer that couldn't be refused. Instead of renewing their contract with Georgene Novelties Co., Inc., the Gruelles decided to go with Knickerbocker.

Several changes were made within a year, the most prominent being the change of hair color from orange to red. The eyelashes, noses, and mouths were altered slightly, but the body remained the same. Not only were there more dolls in more sizes, but variations also were added to the line, including pajama bags, lamps, marionettes, and bean bag dolls.

Mouth variations.

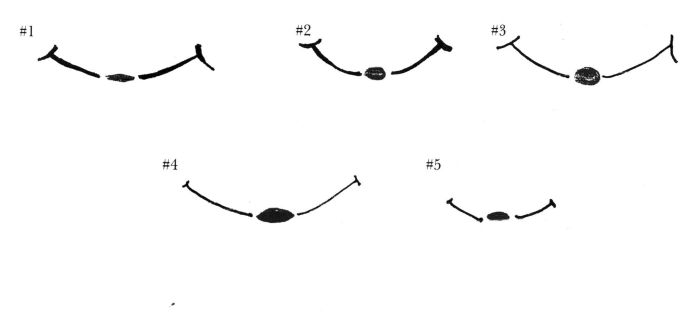

Eyelash variations.

Knickerbocker Toy Co. Tags

(All Knickerbocker tags are attached to the clothing.)
Note: Tags may note a variety of different countries, and
either Andy or Ann.

FRONT
F

> JOHNNY GRUELLE'S OWN
> "RAGGEDY
> ANDY" DOLL
> ©JOHN B. GRUELLE, 1920, 1937
> ©RENEWED BY MYRTLE GRUELLE
> 1945, 1963

(or 1948, 1965)

BACK
F

> JOY OF A TOY
> Knickerbocker
> _____
> KNICKERBOCKER TOY CO. INC.
> MADE IN HONG KONG
> EXCLUSIVE MANUFACTURER

(Could say JAPAN)

FRONT
G

> "RAGGEDY
> ANN" © DOLL
> RAGGEDY ANN DOLL
> ©KNICKERBOCKER TOY CO. INC.
> MIDDLESEX, N.J. 08846 U.S.A.

BACK
G

> JOY OF A TOY
> © Knickerbocker
> _____
> KNICKERBOCKER TOY COMPANY INC.
> MADE IN TAIWAN, REPUBLIC OF CHINA
> EXCLUSIVE MANUFACTURER
> ALL NEW COTTON AND FOAM

FRONT
H

> RAGGEDY
> ANDY ®
> ALL NEW MATERIALS
> STUFFED WITH COTTON

Tags on Andys usually are located on the inside
seam of the pants, or at the back as shown. LEFT:
TAG H. RIGHT: TAG G, 1963-1982.

BACK

H

ᴷᵀᶜ knickerbocker

© KNICKERBOCKER TOY COMPANY INC.
MIDDLESEX, N.J. 08846 U.S.A.
MADE IN TAIWAN REPUBLIC OF CHINA

FRONT

I

RAGGEDY
ANN
ALL NEW MATERIALS
STUFFED WITH COTTON &
SYNTHETIC FIBERS

BACK

I

Joy OF A TOY
Knickerbocker
_____

KNICKERBOCKER TOY COMPANY INC.
MADE IN HONG KONG

FRONT

J

RAGGEDY
ANDY
all new materials
STUFFED WITH COTTON POLYSTYRENE
FOAM AND POLYSTYRENE PELLETS

BACK is the same as H

FRONT

L

RAGGEDY
ANDY
all new materials, colored shredded
clippings, shredded polyurethane
foam, synthetic fibers, and
shredded cellulose fibers
surface washable only

BACK is the same as H

These photos show the variation of hearts in the Knickerbocker line.

Here we see the difference between the earliest 15-in (38-cm) Knickerbocker Andy (TAG F) on the left, and a Georgene Andy 15-in (38-cm) TAG B on the right. Hair color is the same, but there are slight changes in the mouths, noses, and eyebrows.

15-in (38-cm) Raggedy Andy by Knickerbocker Toy Co. These orange-haired dolls were made the first year Knickerbocker took over production. TAG F. 1963-1968. Barbara and Roy Dubay Collection.

Another wonderful Belindy with her original box and tag. Candy Brainard Collection.

These twin sisters both have had their aprons replaced. Barbara and Roy Dubay Collection.

15-in (38-cm) Beloved Belindy by Knickerbocker Toy Co. One-piece dress, pantaloons, and bandanna. Missing apron. This doll was produced at the height of the civil rights movement in 1965. Even though Belindy was a resourceful, creative, and individualistic thinker as portrayed in the Gruelle books, she was deemed offensive and had a short-lived stay on toy store shelves. Even so, they do appear at shows. Tag sewn to the back skirt seam reads: "Beloved Belindy/ Co., Inc. 1965/CAL-T-5 All new material. Joy of a Toy Knickerbocker/Knickbocker Toy Co., Inc., Made in Hong Kong." Author's Collection.

19-in (48-cm) early Knickerbocker pair. Uncommon dress. They have a slight case of dry rot from the sun. TAG C, 1963-1968.

15-in (38-cm) Raggedy Ann and Andy from Knickerbocker Toy Co. These two have tags sewn in their left side seam like the Georgenes. The front is like TAG F, but the back indicates that the dolls were made in New York instead of a foreign country like most other Knickerbockers. Andy has a music box inside which plays Brahms's "Lullaby." All original. Two of the earliest Knickerbockers. 1963-1982.

19-in (48-cm) pair from Knickerbocker Toy Co. Andy is original. Ann's outfit was replaced. Note the thick lines of the mouth. Nice quality dolls. TAG G, 1964.

Two more Anns with their original tags. Barbara and Roy Dubay Collection.

19-in (48-cm) Knickerbocker Andy. This little guy sneaked out of the factory without his hair! The back of his head is solid red. He thinks he's special because he's different. 1963-1982.

15-in (38-cm) Raggedy Andy from Knickerbocker Toy Co. Georgene suit and lambs wool hair. As a novice collector, it was deemed that they may have made dolls with different hair. Little did we know! 1963-1982.

15-in (38-cm) early Knickerbocker Ann with small eyelashes and a thin mouth. This doll, and the two below, have very sweet faces. Their dresses are different. TAG F. She is surrounded by five smaller Raggedys, the far right (lower) made for Hallmark. 1963-1982. Barbara and Roy Dubay Collection.

15-in (38-cm) Ann by Knickerbocker. Very pretty little girl. Nice facial coloring. Made in Taiwan. TAG I, 1963-1982. Author's Collection.

15-in (38-cm) pair of Raggedy Anns from Knickerbocker Toy Co. Early and identical except for the dresses. TAG F.

19-in (48-cm) pair made in Korea by Knicker-bocker Toy Co. TAG F.

Early Knickerbocker pair. Andy's music box plays "Rock-a-bye Baby." TAG F, 1963-1970. Barbara and Roy Dubay Collection.

15-in (38-cm) pair and 19-in (48-cm) Ann by Knickerbocker. Flat-faced dolls made in Korea. Andy has a music box that plays "Frere Jacques." Hair is bright red and quite thick. Different look in the face. TAG F, 1963-1982.

15-in (38-cm) pair by Knickerbocker Toy Co. Andy has a music box inside that plays "Frere Jacques." TAG G. Ann has her original heart tag, plus TAG G on her apron. It says, "stuffed with cotton," but cotton threads can be seen through the fabric. TAG L would have been more accurate. 1963-1982.

19-in (48-cm) pair from Knickerbocker. Like the pair on the left, only taller. Ann has her original tag dated 1964.

15-in (38-cm) pair riding a 1940s stuffed dog with a bell in his ear. Early 1964.

Nice family gathering. Left: 12-in (31-cm) Andy with "Twinkle, Twinkle, Little Star" music box in his tummy. Middle: 15-in (38-cm) Ann from Knickerbocker. Right: 15-in (38-cm) Andy with orange hair like a Georgene. Little bean bag at their feet.

19-in (48-cm) Raggedy Anns from Knickerbocker Toy Co. Same doll, all original, different fabric. The doll at the right has no neck. The area below her mouth is the same width as her head. TAG H, 1963-1982.

19-in (48-cm) Raggedy Anns from Knickerbocker Toy Co. The brown pattern in their dresses also is found as a pajama bag. TAG G, 1963-1982.

19-in (48-cm) Ann. Her brown dress is the same fabric as a pajama bag cataloged as a Christmas item in 1968. Her friend is Raggedy Arthur, also made by Knickerbocker Toy Co. Raggedy Arthur was never a character from Johnny Gruelle's imagination, but was a creation of the Bobbs-Merrill Co., N.Y., in 1965. Barbara and Roy Dubay Collection.

This group of Raggedys couldn't wait to take a ride in this Radio Pal wagon with heart cutout wheels. Barbara and Roy Dubay Collection.

15-in (38-cm) Ann is the mate to the Andy in the gold box. Unusual dress pattern. TAG H, 1963-1982. Barbara and Roy Dubay Collection.

10-in (25-cm) Raggedy Ann and Andy Bean Bags from Knickerbocker Toy Co. Stuffed head and hands, pellet-filled body. Ann has a removable pinafore. TAG J, 1963-1982. Made in China.

6-in (15-cm) Raggedy Ann Lamp. Knickerbocker Toy Co.

Raggedy Andy Lamp by Knickerbocker Toy Co.

Raggedy Andy Lamp. Raggedy is mounted on a plastic block base. TAG H, 1963-1982.

18-in (46-cm) Talking Raggedy Ann and Andy from Knickerbocker Toy Co. Note Ann's purple dress (full view of dolls on page 88). These talkers say a variety of phrases in sweet child voices by pulling a string at the base of the neck. The head and torsos seem slightly larger than other dolls of the same height. 1965.

Talking mechanism found in the torso of the doll. The far right show the little record which is activated and spins when the string is pulled. Phrases include: "I'm Raggedy Andy," "I'm Raggedy Ann," "My friend is Raggedy Ann," "Be kind to everyone," "You're my best friend," "I like talking to you," "I like to be hugged," "Let's play together," "See my candy heart," "I love you so much," "Give me a big hug." The "talkers" were made only for a short time because the mechanism was too complicated and expensive to produce for sale at a reasonable price.

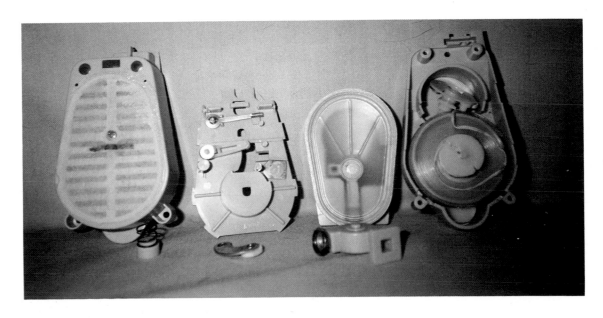

24-in (61-cm) Raggedy Andys from Knickerbocker Toy Co. Identical except for shirt. They're enjoying the company of "Bunky," their favorite English bear.

15-in (38-cm) pair by Knickerbockers love the little camel. They have bright red hair and lovely faces. These dolls were made in Malaysia, and they are distinctly different up close. TAG H,1963-1982.

11-in (28-cm) Camel with the Wrinkled Knees from Knickerbocker Toy Co. Often when Johnny Gruelle returned from his trips to New York, he brought toys for his children. One time a cute, white camel was tucked under his arm. Very shortly after the camel had been bounced across the kitchen table, the fabric wore through on each foot, and Gruelle withdrew a long skewer from each leg! As the legs started to collapse, creativity took over, and the Camel with the Wrinkled Knees was born. The original white color was later changed to blue because it photographed better for an early movie.

24-in (61-cm) Raggedy Anns from Knickerbocker
Toy Co. Similar except for their dresses. Lower
left doll has larger eyes. TAG G, 1963-1975.

19-in (48-cm) Raggedy Anns and 15-in (38-cm)
Raggedy Andy from Knickerbocker. Typical late
1960s and early 1970s dolls. Other Ann is TAG G,
1963-1982.

30-in (76-cm) Raggedy Ann from Knickerbocker Toy Co. Big sister to the standing doll. Purple
and blue flowered dress. TAG G, 1963-1975. Private Collection.

Talkers. Full view of the dolls described (on page 85). Wider and fatter than the usual Raggedys to accommodate the mechanism. TAG G, 1965.

12-in (31-cm) Marionette by Knickerbocker. Removable skirt and apron. There are levers on the top panel so that each finger controls a string. TAG H, 1963-1982.

18 1/2-in (47-cm) Raggedy Ann and Andy from Knickerbocker Toy Co. Mint pair made in Taiwan, Republic of China. TAG G, 1963-1982.

6-in (15-cm) Beanbags by Co. Reg. No. 219CR16113. Filled with plastic pellets. Made in Japan. They are joined by the 6-in (15-cm) Knickerbocker Huggies.

6-in (15-cm) Huggies by Knickerbocker Toy Co. Stuffed with cotton. The elongated arms may be slipped over the head to separate the couple, but they look so loving together. TAG H, 1963-1982. Barbara and Roy Dubay Collection.

24-in (61-cm) Dress-Me Dolls by Knickerbocker Toy Co. These wide, unjointed dolls were designed to help young children develop skills with buttons, zippers, snaps, ties, and buckles. Ann has a teddy with laces, a dress that buttons, an apron that zips, and shoes that buckle. Andy's has a shirt that buttons, a tie that forms a bow, a belt that buckles, shoes that tie, and pants that zip. No yarn on the back of the heads. TAG G, 1963-1970.

19-in (48-cm) Ann. This dress can be found on two sizes manufactured in 1971. It has a plain-blue attached skirt, a flowered top, and a flower on the pocket of the apron. Although this doll is mint, there is no tag attached to the apron. Square TAG H, 1971.

15-in (38-cm) Raggedy Andy from Knicker-bocker Toy Co. MIB TAG H, 1963-1982.

15-in (38-cm) Raggedy Ann and Andy from Knickerbocker Toy Co. Flat faces, mint condition. Note how the light picks up the highlights in the eyes. This look is far more natural than painting dots on the buttons, as in later dolls by Knickerbocker. TAG H, 1963-1982.

15-in (38-cm) Raggedy Ann and Andy from Knickerbocker Toy Co. I call these my "Vidal Sassoon" dolls because they look like they just stepped out of the beauty parlor. TAG G, 1963-1982.

19-in (48-cm) Knickerbocker Andy. Oh wow! Out of the whole family, this Andy probably would make the best punk rocker because his hair already is two-toned blonde and orange! Replaced outfit.

15-in (38-cm) Ann has two different hair colors. Maybe she had it frosted! No tag, 1963-1982.

19-in (48-cm) Raggedy Ann from Knickerbocker Toy Co. Flat face, mint condition. TAG H, 1963-1982.

12-in (31-cm) pair by Knickerbocker Toy Co. Music box inside Andy plays an "oriental" version of "Twinkle, Twinkle, Little Star" in a minor key. No tags, 1963-1982.

9-in (23-cm) Bend-em Raggedy Ann from Knickerbocker. Stuffed head, wires in the rest of the body. Very Poor quality. Extra large feet. Yarn hair. Tag states "Made in Japan." No date.

28-in (71-cm) Raggedy Ann Pajama Bag from Knickerbocker Toy Co. Stuffed head, legs, and hands. Zipper down the back. Button eyes, looped orange hair around the seam only. Brown flowered fabric also found on an Ann doll. Late 1960s.

52-in (132-cm) Sleeping Bag. Tag at neck states "Made in Jamaica." Made be made by Knickerbocker and Bobbs-Merrill Co. Child crawls inside the dress and uses the head for a pillow. Different fabrics were used. Orange yarn hair around the edge of the pillow. 1963-1982.

36-in (91-cm) three Knickerbocker Raggedys.
Ann on the left has a different dress from the one
on the right. All are TAG G, 1963-1982.

40-in (102-cm) reworked Knickerbocker Ann.
Replaced arms and legs because insects had
destroyed them.

30-in (76-cm) an odd Andy with a thin head and
shorter hair than most. TAG G, 1963-1982.

31 1/2-in (80-cm) Raggedy Ann from Knickerbocker Toy Co. It is always great to find one of these larger dolls with the box. Mint. TAG H, 1963-1982.

31 1/2-in (80-cm) Raggedy Andy from Knickerbocker Toy Co. Although not purchased together, he is the mate to Ann on the left. TAG H, 1963-1982.

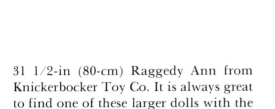

Bedtime Raggedy Ann and Andy from Knickerbocker. Soft baby toy, flannel pajamas and nightie, no button eyes. Pictured in Hasbro 1984 catalog. 1979-1982.

Hand Puppets from Knickerbocker. TAG H. Bend-em Raggedy in the middle. Knickerbocker Toy Co. TAG F, 1962-1982.

40-in (102-cm) Raggedy Ann by Knickerbocker. This young lady came with a veil and bouquet of flowers because she was the center of attention at a bridal shower. Her pink dress matches the lovely Royal Bonn mantle clock. No tag, 1963-1982.

40-in (102-cm) Andy by Knickerbocker. Mate to Ann on left. Well constructed of good quality materials. TAG H, 1963-1982.

Knickerbocker Ann made in Haiti. Strange face. Machine washable. TAG: "Knickerbocker/So-Soft/Baby Toys." 1978-1982.

36-in (91-cm) Raggedy Andy. He would make a perfect match for this "Annie" if they didn't live in two different states. Barbara and Roy Dubay Collection.

36-in (91-cm) Raggedy Ann from Knickerbocker Toy Co. Mint with tag. She's beautiful! TAG H, 1963-1982.

78-in (198-cm) Raggedy Ann and Andy by Knickerbocker Toy Co. They probably were made for a store display with the smaller dolls sitting around them, or perhaps for a display float. 1963-1982. Candy Brainard Collection.

45-in (114-cm) pair spent so much time jumping in and out of the cars that we could hardly get them to sit still for a formal portrait!

45-in (114-cm) Raggedy Anns by Knickerbocker Toy Co. To the right is "Big Annie." Her five eyelashes, instead of the typical four, give her a very kind look. She's one of our favorites, and she knows it! Her sister to the left is identical except for her yellow-, green-, and blue-flowered dress. Even so, their expressions are different. TAG H, 1963-1982.

45-in (114-cm) Raggedy Andy by Knickerbocker Toy Co. MIB, Jean Bach, formerly of the Raggedy Ann Doll Museum in Flemington. N.J., used to tell stories to school and neighborhood groups "through" his sister, Ann. Andy never was used for this purpose, and finding a doll this big in the box was a big thrill! TAG H, 1963-1982.

Barbara and Roy Dubay also have this big boy who loves to get into all kinds of mischief, including climbing trees.

All the dolls on this page were made for a short time by Knickerbocker Toy Co. around 1976. Most change is noticed in the eyelashes, mouths, and outfits. The pair (above left) is 15-in (38-cm) tall. Above right are 5-in (13-cm) tall; and the two Andys below are 19-in (48-cm) each. Andy on the bottom right would have been sold as a duplicate until the "Raggedy Ann" tag was noticed! TAG L, circa 1976 for all.

This trunk-shaped humidor is packed with Raggedys from the 1973 to 1976 era. They range in size from 3-in (7 1/2-cm) to 24-in (61-cm). TAG L. Barbara and Roy Dubay Collection.

30-in (76-cm) Raggedy Ann by Knickerbocker Toy Co. Later dolls can be identified by the close-set eyelashes and the thin mouth. TAG L, 1976-1982.

40-in (102-cm) Ann by Knickerbocker. Blue and red polka-dot dress. TAG L, 1973-1982.

18-in (46-cm) Andy by Knickerbocker. Made around 1973. Unusual aqua-color outfit. TAG I.

6-in (15-cm) pillow-type Knickerbockers. Seam separates soft body from pellet feet. TAG H, 1963-1982.

40-in (102-cm) Raggedy Ann and Andy by Knickerbocker Toy Co. "Jenny" (the cat) almost sat on Andy's lap. These big dolls came out in the mid-1970s. Andy's outfit probably is fashioned after a similar one illustrated in several of the Raggedy books. Small eyelashes and mouth. Both are mint. 1976.

A very happy duo, consisting of Raggedy Arthur and the Camel with the Wrinkled Knees. These accessory animals were made by Knickerbocker in 1965. Barbara and Roy Dubay Collection.

19-in (48-cm) pair. TAG L for all.

Box for the 35-inch Ann and Andy

These dolls all were made by Knickerbocker Toy Co. during their last few years in business from 1978 to 1982. They all have bright red hair of an acrylic fiber, tiny eyelashes, and the same outfits. The largest size has white dots to highlight the button eyes. Boxes for 35-inch Raggedys by Knickerbocker Toy Co. 1979-1982.

35-in (89-cm) pair.

12-in (31-cm) Annie hardly could stay in her box.

36-in (91-cm) Raggedy Andy by Applause. Embroidered face and button. 1981.

36-in (91-cm) Raggedy Ann by Applause. A transition doll from Knickerbocker to Applause, which began as a division of Knickerbocker. Applause doll, labeled Knickerbocker dress. 1981.

Applause Toy Company 1981-1983 and Hasbro Company 1983-Present

The Applause Toy Company began as a division of Knickerbocker Toy Co. in 1979. Knickerbocker was a subsidiary of Warner Communications and sold their toy line through Toys 'R Us stores. Applause, on the other hand, was a gift line marketed through Hallmark. Applause merged with Wallace-Barrie in the early 1980s and presently does its licensing through Hasbro Company in Pawtucket, Rhode Island.

The license for these dolls is owned by Worth Gruelle, John B. Gruelle's son, and has the John B. Gruelle copyright. Knickerbocker was bought by Hasbro in 1983.

Applause catalogs note that they produced embroidery-faced dolls in four sizes: 12-inch (31-cm), 17-inch (43-cm), 25-inch (64-cm), and 36-inch (91-cm) in both 1981 and 1982. The 1982 Christmas catalog shows a prepackaged pair with holly on Andy's hat and Ann's pinafore. This same 12-inch pair was featured for Valentine's Day in 1984 wearing red-heart-covered material for the shirt and dress. Only this size of dolls ever are found in boxes, and always in pairs. The other sizes are packed in large boxes of a dozen for shipping only.

In 1986, Macmillan Publishing Company also bought the rights to make certain Raggedy products, including hand puppets and silk-screened dolls with music boxes in them. They play 'Raindrops Keep Fallin' on My Head' and 'I'd Like to Teach the World to Sing.' By April 1989, they released a new line of children's grooming aids.

25-in (64-cm) pair by Applause, a division of Knickerbocker Toy Co. Andy is No. 8459, Ann is No. 8458. 1981.

Group portrait of the five sizes of Applause Raggedy Anns. 8-in (20-cm), 12-in (31-cm), 17-in (43-cm), 25-in (64-cm), and 36-in (91-cm). 1981.

Group portrait of the Applause Raggedy Andys. 1981.

Valentine Raggedy Ann and Andy from Applause, then a division of Knickerbocker. Heart pattern on shirt and dress. These dolls are listed in the 1984 catalog.

17-in (43-cm) Classic Raggedy Ann and Andy from Applause. A recreation of an earlier Knickerbocker doll with clothes similar to those of Georgenes. Trademark by Johnny Gruelle, Macmillan, Inc. 1987. Private Collection.

48-in (122-cm) Dancing Raggedy Ann from Applause. Doll has loop under its feet so that a child of similar size can dance with it. Circular embroidered eyes appear strange compared to the usual Applause eyes. Mark: "Raggedy Ann and Andy by Johnny Gruelle, © 1986 Macmillan, Inc."

12-in (31-cm) Musical pair by Applause, Macmillan, Inc. Silk-screened faces, no hearts. Ann plays "I'd Like to Teach the World to Sing"; Andy plays "Raindrops Keep Falling on My Head." Windup; body moves as music plays. Currently available. 1987.

12-in (31-cm) pair and 18-in (46-cm) Ann by Hasbro Softies Industries. Copyright by Johnny Gruelle. All new materials, synthetics and cellulose fibers. Sewn in China, assembled in Hong Kong. 1983. MIB.

12-in (31-cm) Raggedy Anns by Hasbro. Both dolls were packed in the same style box, although their faces are decidedly different. Identical clothing. 1983. Doll on the right is currently available under the Playskool label, which is a division of Hasbro.

Story Books

Originally, Johnny Gruelle's main concentration was to find ways to promote his series of children's books. The Raggedy doll was to be merely a prop to help focus the public on his written work. But, the idea of sitting a few dolls around the display soon backfired. He was immediately swamped with orders for the dolls!

Before these first books were published, Johnny already had a following for his written and artistic talent through local newspapers. In the early 1920s there was also a feature entitled "The Adventures of Raggedy Ann and Raggedy Andy." Ann and Andy made it to the movies, too! In 1918 a black-and-white silent film entitled "Raggedy Ann" starred Priscilla Dean and was directed by Tad Browning. In 1941, Paramount Pictures released a color cartoon entitled "Raggedy Ann."

In 1934 the Johnny Gruelle Company was formed by incorporating Myrtle Gruelle, Richard Gruelle, and publisher Howard Cox.

Johnny Gruelle's writing is very sensitive in nature, and has an underlying theme of nonviolence. Through the use of fantasy, Johnny Gruelle enables the reader to share even the most delicate of feelings, as seen, for example, with the fairies in *Marcella*. His approach to the handicap and eventual death of a small boy, and at the same time the continuance of life with the birth of a puppy, truly is commendable.

A statement found at the end of the early books says, "It is the Gruelle ideal that books for children should contain nothing to cause fright, suggest fear, glorify mischief, excuse malice, or condone cruelty. That is why they are called 'BOOKS GOOD FOR CHILDREN.'"

Raggedy Andy Stories, P.F. Volland Co., 1920. Later 1947, 1948. *Raggedy Ann Stories*, M.A. Donohue Co., 1918. Later 1946, 1947.

Books Written and Illustrated by Johnny Gruelle.

1916   *Rhymes for Kindly Children*--P.F. Volland Co. Written by Ethel Fairmont. Illustrated by Johnny Gruelle.

1917   *Raggedy Ann and Andy's Very Own Fairy Stories*--P.F. Volland Co., 1917, 1945; Myrtle Gruelle, 1949.

1918   *Raggedy Ann Stories*--M.A. Donohue Co., 1918, 1946, 1947; Bobbs-Merrill Co., 1961.

1919   *The Friendly Fairies*--P.F. Volland Co.; Bobbs-Merrill Co., 1960.

1920   *Raggedy Andy Stories*--P.F. Volland Co., 1920, 1947, 1948; Bobbs-Merrill Co., 1960.

1920   *Johnny Mouse and the Wishing Stick*--Bobbs-Merrill Co., 1920, 1921, 1922.

1921   *Eddie Elephant*--P.F. Volland Co.

1922   *Man in the Moon Stories*--Cupples and Leon Co. Illustrated by Johnny Gruelle.

1924   *The Camel with the Wrinkled Knees*--J. Gruelle; Myrtle Gruelle, 1951; Bobbs-Merrill Co., 1960.

1925   *Raggedy Ann Wishing Pebbles*--P.F. Volland Co.

1925   *Raggedy Ann and Andy Alphabet Numbers*--P.F. Volland Co., 1924, 1925; Myrtle Gruelle, 1952, 1957; Bobbs-Merrill Co., 1972.

1926   *Beloved Belindy*--P.F. Volland Co., 1936, 1941; Myrtle Gruelle, 1953; Bobbs-Merrill Co., 1960.
        Raggedy Ann and the Paper Dragon--P.F. Volland Co.; Myrtle Gruelle, 1953; Bobbs-Merrill Co., 1972.

1927   *Wooden Willie*--P.F. Volland Co., 1927; Donohue Co., 1954.

1928   *Raggedy Ann's Magical Wishes*--M.A. Donohue Co.
        My Very Own Fairy Stories

1929   *Marcella*--J. Gruelle Co.
        The Cheery Scarecrow--J. Gruelle, 1929.

1930   *Raggedy Ann in the Deep, Deep Woods*--J. Gruelle.
        The Gingerbread Man--Whitman Pub. Co. Written by Josephine Laurence. Illustrated by Johnny Gruelle.

1931   *Raggedy Ann in Cookieland*--J. Gruelle, 1931; Bobbs-Merrill Co., 1960.

1932   *Raggedy Ann's Lucky Pennies*--J. Gruelle.

1935   *Raggedys Ann's Alphabet Book*
        Raggedy Ann and the Left-Handed Safety Pin

1939   *Raggedy Ann in the Magic Book*--J. Gruelle Co., 1939; Bobbs-Merrill Co., 1961. Illustrated by Worth Gruelle.

1940   *Raggedy Ann and the Golden Butterfly*--J. Gruelle Co.

1941   *Raggedy Andy in the Garden*
        Raggedy Andy Goes Sailing

1942   *The Nice Fat Policeman*--J. Gruelle. Illustrated by Worth Gruelle.

1943   *Raggedy Ann and Betsy Bonnet String*--J. Gruelle Co. Illustrated by Justin Gruelle.
        Raggedy Ann Helps Grandpa Hoppergrass
        Raggedy Ann and the Happy Toad

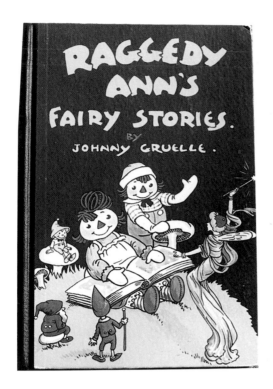

Raggedy Ann's Fairy Stories, 1917.

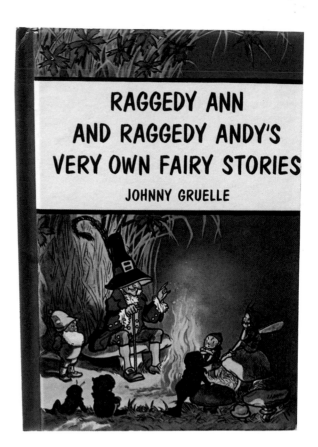

Raggedy Ann and Raggedy Andy's Very Own Fairy Stories, P.F. Volland Co., 1917, 1945; Myrtle Gruelle, 1949.

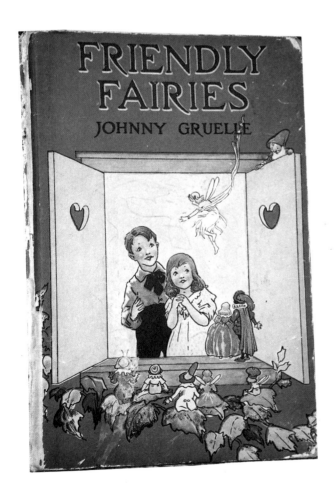

The Friendly Fairies, P.F. Volland Co., 1919.

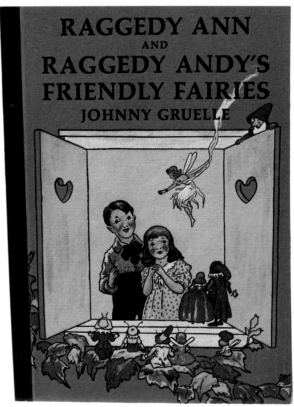

Later edition of *The Friendly Fairies,* Bobbs-Merrill Co., 1960.

Camel with the Wrinkled Knees, Johnny Gruelle Co., 1924; Myrtle Gruelle, 1951; Bobbs-Merrill Co., 1960.

Raggedy Ann's Wishing Pebbles, P.F. Volland Co., 1925.

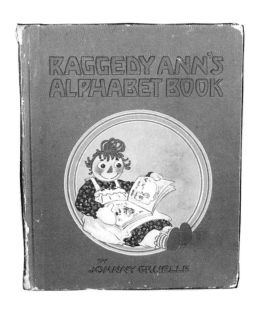

Beloved Belindy, P.F. Volland Co., 1926, 1941; Myrtle Gruelle, 1953; Bobbs-Merrill Co., 1960. The original box for one of the early books always is something special.

Raggedy Ann's Alphabet Book, P.F. Volland Co., 1925.

Raggedy Ann's *Magical Wishes*, 1928.

Raggedy Ann and the Paper Dragon, P.F. Volland
Co., 1926; Myrtle Gruelle, 1953; Bobbs-Merrill
Co., 1972.

Wooden Willie, P.F. Volland Co., 1927.
Donohue Pub., 1954.

Marcella by Johnny Gruelle. J.B. Gruelle Co., 1929.

Raggedy Ann in the Deep, Deep Woods, Johnny
Gruelle, 1930.

Raggedy Ann in Cookieland. Johnny Gruelle,
1931; Bobbs-Merrill Co., 1960.

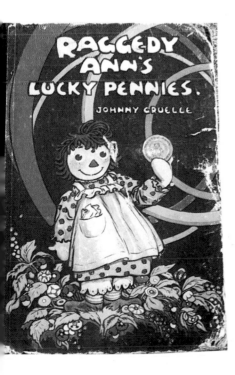

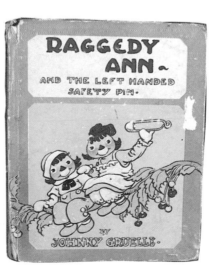

*Raggedy Ann and the Left-handed
SAfety Pin,* 1935.

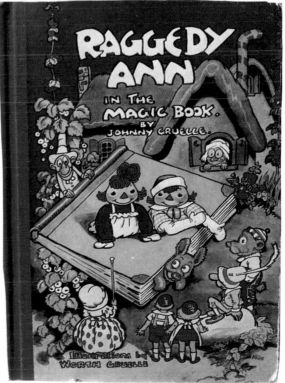

Raggedy Ann's Lucky Pennies, 1932.

Raggedy Ann in the Magic Book, Johnny Gruelle
Co., 1939. Illustrated by Worth Gruelle.

Raggedy Ann and the Golden Butterfly, Johnny Gruelle Co., 1940.

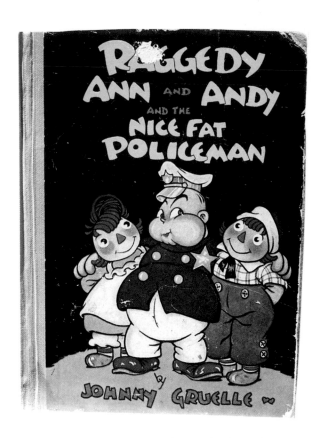

Raggedy Ann and Andy and the Nice Fat Policeman, Johnny Gruelle, 1942. Illustrated by Worth Gruelle.

Raggedy Ann and Betsy Bonnet String, Johnny Gruelle, 1943. Illustrated by Justin Gruelle.

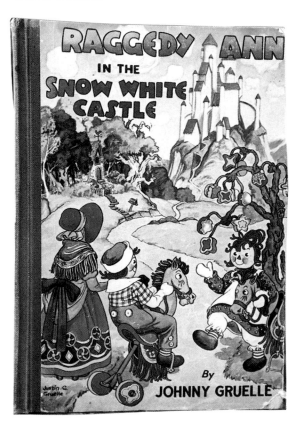

Raggedy Ann in the Snow White Castle, Johnny Gruelle, 1946.

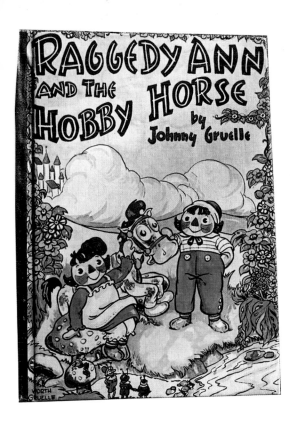

Raggedy Ann and the Hobby Horse, Bobbs-Merrill Co., 1961. Illustrated by Worth Gruelle.

Raggedy Ann and the Happy Meadow, 1961.

Raggedy Ann and the Wonderful Witch. Illustrated by Worth Gruelle. Bobbs-Merrill Co., 1961.

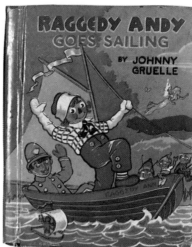
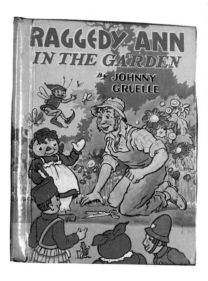

Raggedy Andy Goes Sailing, 1941.

Raggedy Ann in the Garden, 1941.

Raggedy Ann Helps Grandpa Hoppergrass and
Camel with the Wrinkled Knees McLaughlin
Bros., 1943.

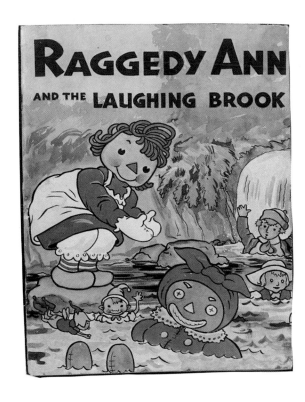

Raggedy Ann and the Laughing Brook by J. Gruelle and John Sherman Bagg. Drawings by Mary and Wallace Stoner after Gruelle. 1944.

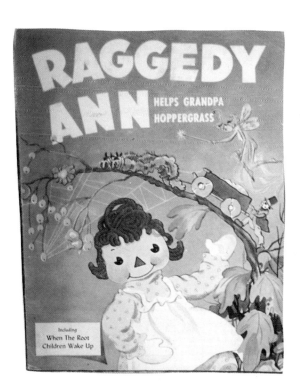

Raggedy Ann Helps Grandpa Hoppergrass and *Raggedy Ann in the Garden* by Johnny Gruelle. Illustrations by Mary and Wallace Stover after Gruelle. Perks Publishing. Copyright by John S. Bagg. 1946.

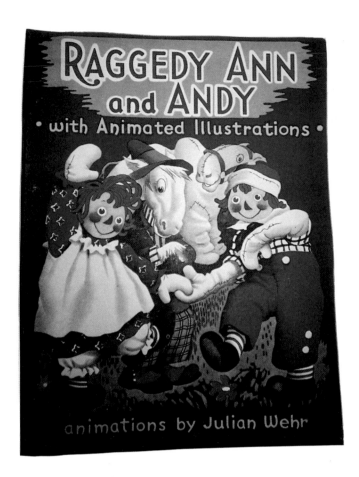

Raggedy Ann and Andy. Animated illustrations by Julian Wehr, Saalfield Publishing Co. Copyright by Johnny Gruelle Co. Scenes in the story are animated by pulling tabs which make part of the picture move. 1944.

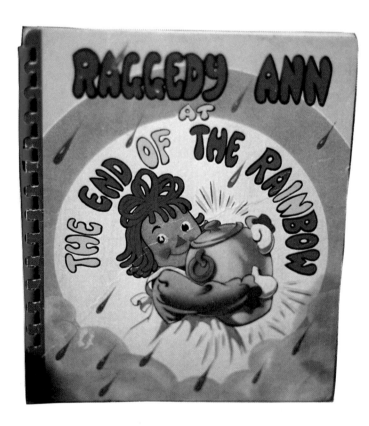

Raggedy Ann at the End of the Rainbow. by Johnny Gruelle. Drawings by Ethel Hays. Saalfield Publishing Co., 1947.

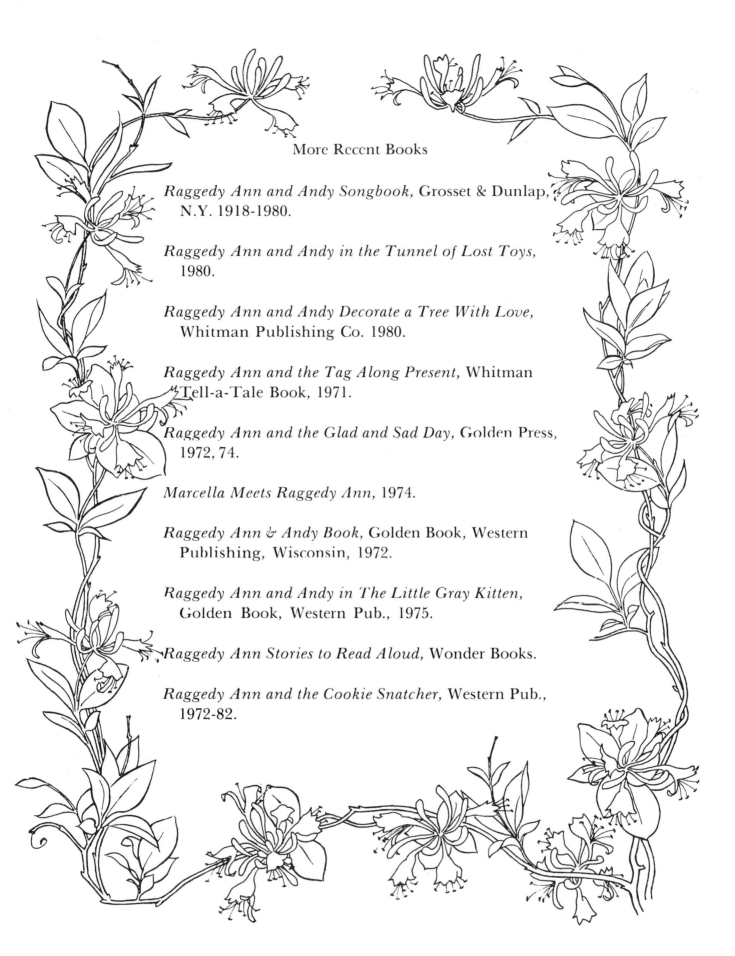

More Recent Books

Raggedy Ann and Andy Songbook, Grosset & Dunlap, N.Y. 1918-1980.

Raggedy Ann and Andy in the Tunnel of Lost Toys, 1980.

Raggedy Ann and Andy Decorate a Tree With Love, Whitman Publishing Co. 1980.

Raggedy Ann and the Tag Along Present, Whitman Tell-a-Tale Book, 1971.

Raggedy Ann and the Glad and Sad Day, Golden Press, 1972, 74.

Marcella Meets Raggedy Ann, 1974.

Raggedy Ann & Andy Book, Golden Book, Western Publishing, Wisconsin, 1972.

Raggedy Ann and Andy in The Little Gray Kitten, Golden Book, Western Pub., 1975.

Raggedy Ann Stories to Read Aloud, Wonder Books.

Raggedy Ann and the Cookie Snatcher, Western Pub., 1972-82.

Here are several examples of pillows made from kits over the years. Since there are no visible tags, we can make the safe assumption that most are Bobbs-Merrill Co. They vary from 6-in (15-cm) to 16-in (41-cm).

Associated Items

There is enough evidence to believe that accessory items began to appear on the market shortly after the first dolls went into mass production. The September 1931 issue of *Playthings* magazine displayed a group of stuffed Gruelle characters which included Uncle Clem, Percy the Policeman, Beloved Belindy, the Little Brown Bear, Johnny Mouse, Cleety the Clown, Sunny Bunny, and Eddie Elephant. Here is a list of several Raggedy Ann and Andy items, other than dolls, that still can be found at flea markets and yard sales. Hundreds of these accessories have been made over the years.

playing cards	pajama bag	lamps
banks	curtains	pencil set
sheets	baby ball	rocking chair
playpen	change purse	pocketbook
toy box	quilt	puzzles
blanket	dishes	rugs
'snow balls'	pillows	desk set
electric toothbrush	prints	sheet music
puppets	song books	radio
music boxes	Halloween costumes	colorforms
sleeping bag	paper dolls	blackboard
waste basket	squeaky toys	TV chair

The March 1941 *Playthings* article, 'Raggedy Ann Comes Into Her Own' listed many companies licensed through William C. Erskine, 9 Rockefeller Plaza, New York, N.Y. for the Johnny Gruelle Company. They include:

Barr Rubber Products	balloons
Milton Bradley Company	games, bubble sets
Collegeville Flag and Manufacturing Company	costumes
M.A. Donohue	books
Fisher Price	toys
Georgene Novelties Company, Incorporated	dolls (retailing for two dollars each!)
Halsam Products Company	building blocks
Miller Music Company	music
P.F. Volland Publishing Company	greeting cards

There also were several other companies added to the list.

Talking Alarm Clock, Janex Corp. Made in Hong Kong, 1974.

Raggedy Ann High Chair, Bobbs-Merrill Co. No date.

Wood blocks. 1930's. Mint In Box. Candy Brainard Collection.

Child's Rocking Chair. Fabric with older-looking Raggedy and her wonderful top knot.

Raggedy Ann and Andy "Talking Bank" by Janex Corp. Battery operated bank has two separate series of coin slots at the top--one for each figure. When coin is dropped in Andy's side, he says, "Don't listen to Ann...Give me your money." Ann says, "Don't give your coins to Andy... He'll spend it on popcorn and candy." Copyright1977, Bobbs-Merrill Co.

Raggedy Ann Sew-Ons Colorforms. Norwood, N.J. and Bobbs-Merrill Co. Different outfits are laced on to forms with yarn shoestrings. 1976.

Raggedy Ann Dress-Up Kit. Bobbs-Merrill Co. "Color forms and plastic pieces stick like magic." 1967.

A Raggedy Ann Song Book. A record of children's songs by Richard Wolfe. RCA. 1971.

Raggedy Ann and Andy Birthday Party record, with Bobbs-Merrill characters.

Raggedy Ann Cut Out Dolls by Johnny Gruelle. Milton Bradley Co., 1941. Kathy George Collection.

Raggedy Ann Paper Dolls, #369 Saalfield Publishing Co., 1944. Kathy George Collection.

Raggedy Ann and Andy Paper Dolls. Ethel Simms, artist. Saalfield Publishing Co., 1957. Kathy George Collection.

Aunt Belindy Picture Puzzles. Madmar Quality.
Two puzzles enclosed. Mid-1930s.

Raggedy Ann Picture Puzzles. Copyright by Johnny
Gruelle. Contains four complete puzzles the size
of the box (10 1/2 x 14 inches). Worth Gruelle
designed these puzzles, although he was not given
credit for them. John Gruelle had died in 1938,
and these were produced in 1940. Milton Bradley
Co.

Raggedy Ann Picture Puzzle. Madmar Quality.
Still sealed in cellophane.

The Games of Raggedy Ann, illustrated by Worth Gruelle. Milton Bradley Co., 1940. Kathy George Collection.

Raggedy Ann's Magic Pebble Game. Copyright by Johnny Gruelle Co. and Milton Bradley Co. Illustrations by Worth Gruelle. 1941.

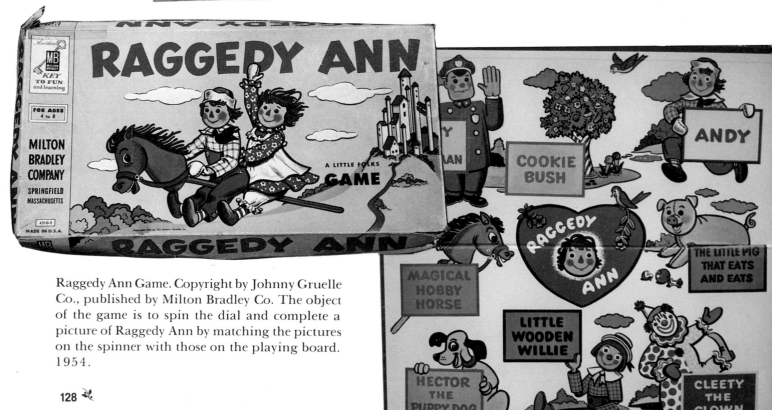

Raggedy Ann Game. Copyright by Johnny Gruelle Co., published by Milton Bradley Co. The object of the game is to spin the dial and complete a picture of Raggedy Ann by matching the pictures on the spinner with those on the playing board. 1954.

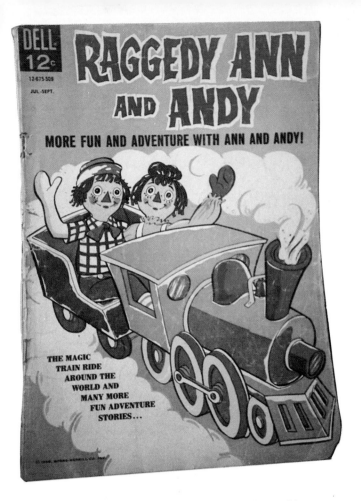

Raggedy Ann and Andy Comic Book. Bobbs-Merrill Co. No 2, July-September 1965. Contains a group of short stories.

"Raggedy Ann's Joyful Songs" by Johnny Gruelle and Charles Miller. Copyright 1937 by Miller Music Corporation. The first collection of Raggedy Ann songs was published in 1930. This book was the author's second joint venture.

"In Love with Love" sheet music from "The Stepping Stones" by Anne Caldwell and Jerome Kern. There are at least four, maybe six, individual songs from this show that were published as sheet music. Cover is a duplicate of the book cover of Raggedy Andy Stories by Johnny Gruelle. Dated 1923.

Raggedy Ann's Sunny Songs by Johnny Gruelle and Will Woodin. Kathy George Collection.

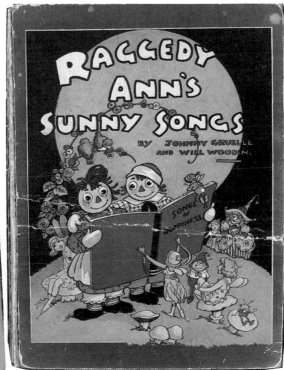

Raggedy Ann Coloring Book, shown with a group of Anns.

Cleety the Clown's Coloring Book, by Johnny Gruelle. Saalfield Publishing Co., 1945. Kathy George Collection.

Raggedy Ann and Raggedy Andy, 4 Books to Color, by J. Gruelle. Saalfield Publishing Co., 1945. Kathy George Collection.

Ceramic Dish and Mug, unmarked. Raggedy Ann and Andy are riding a checkered horse, one of the characters in the Gruelle books. Late 1930s to early 1940s.

Plate to a child's plastic set that included two bowls and a mug. Each piece has a different scene with a lot of detail. Marked Bobbs-Merrill Co., 1969.

Watering Can by Bobbs-Merrill Co., 1971.

Puffy print of Raggedy Andy by Artograph Co. Date is 1942 (under frame).

Kaleidoscope. Image of Raggedy Ann appears with each change of the tube. Bobbs-Merrill Co., 1964. Barbara and Roy Dubay Collection.

6-in (15-cm) Squeak Toy marked "Myrtle Gruelle" on the back.

9-in (23-cm) Combination Squeak Toy and Bank. Marked Myrtle Gruelle. Bobbs-Merrill Co.

11-in (28-cm) Raggedy Squeak Toy. Marked: "Mfg. by Arrow Industries, Bobbs-Merrill Co." 1965.

Pair of Finger Puppets by Knickerbocker and Bobbs-Merrill Co. 4-in (10-cm) jointed vinyl doll with removable cloth dress. Unmarked. 1972.

24-in (61-cm) Raggedy Ann by Nasco Doll Inc.; Bobbs-Merrill Co. Standard-jointed hard-plastic doll body with a Raggedy head. Stamped features. Removable clothes. Marked: 'Raggedy Ann' on the apron. 1972.

30-in (76-cm) Ventriloquist Dummies by Bobbs-Merrill Co. Hard plastic head and hands, foam body, printed face, hair is same length all over the head. 1974.

10-in (25-cm) Standing Banks. Vinyl removable heads, triangular or rectangular noses. Different characters: George and Martha Washington, Cheerleader, Football Player, Paul Revere, Hillbilly, and others. Marked on feet: "Royalty Industries of Fla. Inc. 1974."

10-in (25-cm) George Washington Bank. Royalty Industries. 1974.

6-in (15-cm) Raggedy Andy Bank. Two-piece ceramic nodder. Hat reads: "a penny saved." Labeled "Japan" on the bottom.

19-in (48-cm) porcelain dolls. Cloth bodies; porcelain hands, feet, and heads. Limited edition 1983 by Ideal Co. Barbara and Roy Dubay Collection.

Three rubber Bend-ees dolls. Made of rubber with wires throughout the body. Andy is 6-in (15-cm). Marked: "1978 Bobbs-Merrill Inc., Amscan, Inc. Harrison, N.Y. Made in Hong Kong. Item no. 44015/99." 5 1/2-in (13-cm) Ann. Marked: "1967 Bobbs-Merrill. Mfg. by Lakeside Inc." 2 1/2-in (7-cm) Ann. Marked: "T.B.M. Co. Inc. Hong Kong."

15-in (38-cm) Raggedy Ann Purse by Bobbs-Merrill Co. Padded head, cardboard in legs, two pockets in apron, zipper in back of dress. On tag: "Mini-Clothes by Giftique. N.Y. Handmade in Republic of Philippines. 1977."

Close-up of the Marcella doll.

17-in (43-cm) Marcella doll by Wendy Lawton. Beautiful bisque doll fashioned from an etching by Johnny Gruelle of his daughter, Marcella. This is an earlier proof of the final model. Macmillan, Inc. has the rights to this doll at this time. 1987.

This wonderful color drawing by Worth Gruelle is fashioned after an earlier work by his father. The title is "Blue Birds."

Keeping a Collection

Condition

Condition of the Raggedys often can determine the difference between a collection and an accumulation. Rag dolls have many natural enemies: dampness, dirt, cigarettes, pens, and crayons, just to name a few. This is why we rejoice at finding that perfect doll, which for one reason or another has survived the passage of time. Raggedys have been objects of love and hate at the same time, evidenced by the scribbles all over bodies, scissor and pencil punctures, and even missing eyes! While some dolls are in poor condition, others are found with all clothes (even bloomers and hats) intact. Having the complete clothing is just as exciting to the Raggedy collector as finding a more expensive doll in its original attire.

Rehabilitation

Sometimes we all have the desire to give some poor 'unfortunate' a home, no matter how pathetic the doll may appear. Also, the armless doll, no matter how dirty, may be the only example you have been able to locate of a fairly rare Raggedy.

Body

In some cases we have been quite successful in restoring Georgene and hand-made Raggedys, but the job requires much time and patience. Earlier dolls are stuffed with soft, white cotton (sometimes including seeds), while later Knicker-bockers have been found filled with dark, shredded material, such as may be used in upholstery work. It may be that the country of origin used whatever was available at the time.

This "No Hope" doll was found missing an arm and covered with rust. A clean version is shown on page 50. Gwen Daniels Collection.

Once the wig is removed, most Raggedys made after 1940 can be washed. Good judgment must be employed beforehand to insure that the fabric is not dry-rotted from sun exposure and that there are no tears in the body.

Hair

Sewn-on yarn wigs can be removed in seconds, while glued ones are better left untouched. In most cases Ann has a top knot and is slightly taller than her brother. Sometimes the clothes of pairs have been switched, and the top knot (often of a thicker yarn) is a good identifying aid. If all or part of the hair is missing, cotton rug yarn makes an acceptable substitute, unless one is able to locate yarn made years ago.

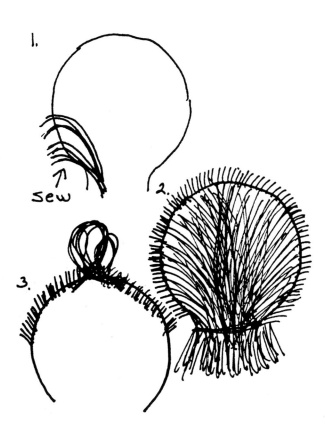

1. Yarn cut in strips can be sewn along the seam joining the front and back of the head, using clumps of six or eight strands. Follow them around the head.

2. Smooth strands and join at the back of the neck in a straight line.

3. Top knot can be added to the top of the head.

4. Trim and shape ends.

Applying yarn by individual knots does not appear as authentic as the above method.

15-in (38-cm) Raggedy Andy, Knickerbocker Toy Co. Hair replaced; early TAG F. WIth him is a Dam Troll Giraffe, 1965.

 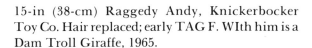

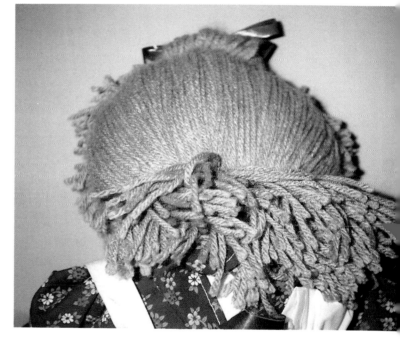

23-in (59-cm) Raggedy Ann by Georgene Novelties Co., Inc. This series of photos illustrates the restoration of a doll purchased for $1.00 at a market. Ann had no clothes, much of her hair was missing, and she was very dirty. The face was repainted after washing and restuffing the body. Her hair was replaced and she has new clothes. Sometimes experimentation is the only way to prove it can be done. Personal judgment must be used in any decision this radical. At least now Annie would be a lovely present for that special little person. Tag missing, 1938-1962.

CAUTION: If you choose to machine-wash the doll, the facial ink probably will fade and the face may need to be repainted. Pre-washing and pre-soaking may help loosen age-old dirt. Chlorine bleach works well, but will fade the flesh tones to white. We've removed the stuffing, but the end result is the same with the stuffing left in the body. Also, restuffing is a tedious process, as the arms and legs have to be removed and resown to the torso.

All of the above procedures work best on later handmade dolls, and are merely suggestions of what can or could be done. Again, judgment is the key word here. Unless there is a severe problem, such as a missing limb, it seems best to leave them as found. I do like to clothe my dolls; however, many collectors have dozens in the buff!

Inventory

As with any collection, it always is advisable to keep an accurate record of each doll you buy. Very soon you will acquire an overall view of the pricing habits in your area. This guide will help you determine which dolls seem to be good buys at the moment.

Any simple ledger could be used as a form for your inventory.

EXAMPLE (Doll)	SIZE	WHERE PURCHASED	WHEN	COST

(This chart may be reproduced for your use.)

Price Guide

P.F. VOLLAND COMPANY—1920 to 1934. Early Raggedy Ann and Andy.
  Original clothes, good condition, slight soil: $1200-850
  Fair condition: $800-750 Poor condition: $350-175
  Beloved Belindy—black or dark brown body, out-turned legs, flowered top, red skirt, organdy apron. Good condition: $1800-700

MOLLYE'S DOLL OUTFITTERS—Mollye Goldman, designer from 1935-1938.
  Signed on front of torso.
  Mollye Baby—14-15 inches (36-38 cm): not enough examples for accurate pricing.
  Ann and Andy—15 inches (38 cm) to 18 inches (46 cm):
    Mint: $700-650 each Good: $600-500 each Fair: $300-150
  Ann and Andy—21-22 inches (53-56 cm):
    Mint: $850 Good: $700 each Fair: $350-175 each

Beloved Belindy—not made commercially by this company, although Mollye did make a doll for her own private collection.

GEORGENE NOVELTIES CO., INC.—1938-1962

	Size	Excellent	Good	Fair
First version	19" (48 cm) Black outlined nose	$750	500	275
1938	50" (127 cm) store display*	NA	NA	NA
After 1940	15" 200	150	85-75	
	19" 250	200-125	125-85	
	23"-24" 325	225	150-125	
	31-36" 415-350	275	200-150	
	45* 850	600-500	275	
1938	18" Beloved Belindy	850-800	600-500	325-150
After 1940	15" Beloved Belindy	775	500	300
	12" Awake-Asleep	375	250	200-150

Prices may be higher for MIB and TAG.

*This size seems quite rare. If on the market, would probably be over $1200. If you can afford it, buy it!

KNICKERBOCKER TOY CO.—1963-1982

	Size	Mint	Good	Fair
Ann/Andy	5" (13)	15	12	8
	8" (20)	22	18	10
	12" (31)	30	25-20	12
	15" (38)	48	40-35	20
	19" (48)	55	42	28-20
	24" (61)	85-75	65	40-32
	30" (76)	125	85-80	65-45
	36" (91)	150	110-95	75-60
	40" (102)	225	150	110
	45 (114)	350	225	150
	78" (198)	NA	NA	NA
Talker (70s)	12" (31)	125	100	50
Talker (60s)	18" (46)	185	150-120	85
Marionette	12" (31)	45	35	25
P.J. Bag	28" (71)	85	60	40
Sleeping Bag	52" (132)	125	95	70-60
Musical	15" (38)	75-65	60-55	40-35
Hand Puppets		30	22	15-12
Bean Bags	10" (25)	28	24	20-18
Bedtime	10" (25)	25	20	15
Beloved Belindy	15" (30)	675	425	225
Camel	11" (28)	175	135	95

Note: NA-there are not enough examples of these huge dolls to get an accurate pricing so, again, if you can afford it, buy it!

APPLAUSE COMPANY—1981-
still available with changes in the embroidered faces.

	Size	1980s	1990s
Ann/Andy	8"	15	12
	12"	25	20-18
Musical	12"	45	—
Ann/Andy	17"	35	25
	25"	85	60-55
	36"	130-125	100
	48"	150	
Camel		35"	22

All dolls in fine condition

HASBRO and PLAYSKOOL—still being manufactured

	Size	Price
Ann/Andy	12	15
Ann/Andy	18	20

Bend-em Raggedy Ann	$12-20
Original book, Johnny Gruelle, 1920s-1940s	35-65
Marcella doll, Wendy Lawton	375
Camel and *Hoppergrass* books 1943	35-48
Animated Illustrations, Julian Wehr	45-75
End of the Rainbow, J. Gruelle and E. Hays	45-65
Raggedy Picture Puzzles (4) 1940	55-85
Belindy Picture Puzzles, 1930s	50-85
Picture Puzzles, Junior Series, 1930s	65-90
Magic Pebble Game, Milton Bradley, 1941	40-75
Print, Artograph Co., 1942	28-40
Canada Dry Advertisement, 1954	12
Raggedy Ann Sew-Ons, 1976	15
Raggedy Ann Dress-Up Kit, 1967	20-25
Raggedy Ann Songbook Record	15
High Chair by Bobbs-Merrill Co.	25-40
Rocking Chair covered in Raggedy material	25-40
Talking Alarm Clock, 1974	25-35
Ventriloquist Dummy, Bobbs-Merrill Co., 1974	75-100
Raggedy Ann Doll, 23 inches, Bobbs-Merrill Co.	75-100
Finger Puppets, Bobbs-Merrill Co., 1972	15
Four-inch vinyl jointed doll	15
Vinyl squeak toys, various sizes	15-25
Standing Bank, Royalty Industries, 1974	25-40
Pillows, assorted kits	15-30
Raggedy Ann Nodder Bank	20-35
Raggedy Ann Game, Milton Bradley, 1954	15-28
Raggedy Ann's Magic Pebble Game, 1941	45-68
Raggedy Ann and Andy Comic Book, 1965	25
Raggedy Ann Helps Grandpa Hoppergrass and	45-55
Raggedy Ann in the Garden, Perks Pub., 1946	
Ceramic bowl, 1940s	48-65
Ceramic mug, 1940s	40-45
Raggedy Ann and Andy Watering Can, Bobbs-Merrill Co.	22
Raggedy Ann's Joyful Songs,	45
Johnny Gruelle and Charles Miller, 1937	
Sheet music from The Stepping Stones, each	10-12
Raggedy Ann Purse, Bobbs-Merrill Co., 1977	12
Four-piece child's serving set, Bobbs-Merrill Co., 1969	25-35
Raggedy Ann Talking Book	20-35
Raggedy Arthur, Knickerbocker Toy	125
Super-Flex Raggedy Ann and Andy, Bobbs-Merrill, 1967	15-30
Raggedy Ann Lamp, Knickerbocker Toy Co.	25-38

Bibliography

Collectible dolls and accessories of the 1920s and 1930s from Sears, Roebuck and Co. catalogs. Edited by Margaret Adams. Dover Publications, Inc., N.Y. 1986.

Knopf Collectors Guide to American Antiques, Dolls by Wendy Lavitt. Alfred A. Knopf Inc., 1983.

Modern Collectors Dolls, third series. Patricia Smith. Collectors Books, 1976.

Modern Collectors Dolls, fourth series. Patricia Smith. Collectors Books, 1979.

Patricia Smith's Doll Values, fifth series. Patricia Smith. Collectors Books, 1987.

Twentieth Century Dolls, Johana Gast Anderton. Wallace-Homestead Book Co., 1974, 1983.

"Johnny Gruelle and the Raggedys" article. Loraine Burdick. From *Book of Collectible Dolls. The Antique Trader Weekly*. Babka Publishing Co., 1976.

"Did You Know That Raggedy Ann Was a Hoosier?" *Indianapolis Magazine*, December 1974.

"Johnny Gruelle and the Raggedys." Celebrity Doll Club, November 1969.

"Raggedy Ann Comes Into Her Own." *Playthings*, March 1941.

"Raggedy Ann--A Classy Doll." Sandra Sher, Museum of California at Oakland, January-February 1989.